FROM VEGAS
TO VICTORY

THE DEATH OF A PROSTITUTE

FROM VEGAS TO VICTORY

THE DEATH OF A PROSTITUTE

JUDY LAMBORN

P.O. Box 62307
Harrisburg, PA 17106
www.impactcommunications.net

From Vegas to Victory: The Death of a Prostitute

Copyright © 2009 by Judy Lamborn

ISBN-10: 0-9742297-3-3

ISBN-13: 978-0-9742297-3-7

Published in Harrisburg, Pennsylvania, by Impact Communications

Website:
www.impactcommunications.net

Mailing Address:
Impact Communications
P.O. Box 62307
Harrisburg, PA 17106-2307

EDITED BY: Vincent M. Newfield
New Fields & Company
P. O. Box 622 • Hillsboro, Missouri 63050
www.preparethewaytoday.org

COVER DESIGN BY: Steve DeShetler
steve@deshetler.com

BACK COVER PHOTOGRAPHY BY: www.blueistudios.com
HAIR BY: Susie Guetschow
MAKEUP BY: Melissa Nelle

Printed in USA

First Edition: IMPG03-18-20090000000-SSO

CONTENTS

INTRODUCTION

Throughout the writing of my story, I have become very aware of my total inadequacy within myself. I have no earthly idea of how to write a book. However, I do know what God has done in my life, and it is at *His* direction that I offer you my written testimony.

In my former life, I worked as a prostitute. The reason I titled this book *From Vegas to Victory: The Death of a Prostitute* is because the woman I was in my former life no longer exists. The Lord has given me a second chance in life and has totally washed my sins away.

It is my prayer that as you read this book, you will realize that God is faithful to stand by you at *all times* regardless of the situation or circumstance. He is ever willing to let you start over again. His mercy is new every morning! He will allow you to make mistakes and then teach you through the consequences of those mistakes. He is the perfect Father and I love Him with all my heart, soul, mind and strength!

Judy Lamborn

Chapter 1

EARLY LIFE

Snapshots of Home, School & Family

I'M ADOPTED

As long as I can remember, I have always known that I was adopted. It has never really been an issue in my life; I just dealt with the fact and saw myself as a little different than most of my friends. Jerry, my one and only sibling who is two years older than me, is also adopted. We were both infants when we were taken in, and although we do not have the same birth parents, we love each other very much. He and his family are a wonderful part of my life today.

Looking back, there were always questions in the back of my mind like, *I wonder if I look like anybody?* and, *Do I have any brothers or sisters?* Sometimes when I saw someone that looked a lot like me, I would wonder whether they might be related to me somehow.

When I became pregnant with my first child, it became necessary to obtain my medical history. I wanted to know if there was anything in my bloodline that I should know about. Being born in California presented a challenge: Adoption records are sealed and you need a court order to open them. Nevertheless, what I was able to find was enough proof for me to know that I didn't have anything to worry about.

According to the adoption agency officials, my birth parents were not planning to marry. So the mere fact that I wasn't aborted was reason enough for me to rejoice! I have never felt rejected or blamed anything on them. My adoptive mom and dad raised me the best way they knew how. I never lacked anything materially; I had a roof over my head, clothes on my back and food in my belly. We went to church every Sunday, and they taught me right from wrong. As far as I knew, it didn't get any better.

Still, I occasionally found myself wondering if my birth parents even remembered me and if they were still alive. After I invited Jesus Christ into my life, I began to wonder about their salvation. I wanted them to know what God had done with the little girl they conceived so many years earlier. I have personally given birth to two babies, and I think it is nearly impossible to forget the day you bring a child into the world—not to mention the nine months you spend bonding with them prior to delivery.

The hope of someday meeting them has been carried with me as long as I can remember. After I became a Christian, I yearned for them to see the wonderful things God had done in my life—to know their two beautiful grandchildren and the wonderful husband I have been blessed with. Although it would be many years, this desire would in part be met one day.

MEET MOM AND DAD

My adoptive dad and mom were hardworking people. They were both born and raised on farms in Northwest Iowa. The work ethic in the Midwest is both disciplined and strong. It requires long hours and hard physical labor, which lends to callused hands, and some-times callused hearts.

Mom was unable to have children due to medical problems. She and Dad were married for fourteen years before they adopted my brother, Jerry, in 1964. Two years later, I came into the picture. So almost suddenly, after fourteen years of having no children, they were thrust into parenthood. My dad was forty-three and my mom was thirty-six at the time.

I am not convinced that any amount of classroom training can prepare a person for parenthood. But since that was all that was available at the time, my parents took advantage of it. Everything they knew about parenting they learned through the Red Cross, the adoption agency and my grandparents. In spite of their inadequacies, I believe with all my heart that my parents loved me as much as they knew how.

Jerry and I were, without a doubt, the cleanest and best dressed kids in southern California in the late 1960s. I know that all my clothes were custom-made from my mom's Singer sewing machine. Quite often my mom and I wore matching dresses to church. As I stated earlier, I do not ever remember wanting for anything materially. We always had bountiful birthdays and Thanksgiving and Christmas celebrations. It appeared on the outside that we were the "perfect" family.

Church on Sunday was mandatory. Mom was the assistant treasurer of the church and sang in the choir, while dad ran the soundboard. I remember going to Sunday school classes and church outings as early as four and five years old. Although we were very active in the church as a family, the Bible was never read in our home nor do I have any memories of any kind of prayer—other than a quick blessing over the food occasionally.

Neither of my parents graduated from high school. They both worked in the public school system in California—my dad as a janitor and my mom as a cafeteria worker. They worked at night and on the weekends fixing up investment properties to rent or sell. They loved antiques and country music. Since they were off most summers, they purchased a motor home for us to travel the country in. I still remember the conversation we had before they bought the motor home: Did we want the motor home or did we want to go to Christian school? (I was 7 or 8 when this happened.) We had gone to Christian school for two years prior to this and it was a costly investment. They would not be able to afford both. Our choice—the motor home.

I believe we traveled through and visited every state in America except Alaska. Thanks to that motor home, I have seen almost all of the natural wonders our beautiful country has to offer. What a wonderful opportunity! In their eyes, my parents were the perfect providers. Unfortunately, they didn't know the importance of teaching children the Word of God because it was not part of their childhood. More than likely, they felt we got all the Bible teaching we needed at church. They also did not know the importance of reinforcing positive behavior and giving children the nurturing they desperately need. This, too, along with outward displays of affection, was also absent in their homes while growing up. It's sad to say, but I was eighteen years old before I heard the precious words "I love you" from my mom. My dad never spoke them to me. If I could share some advice with all parents, I believe it would be, "Tell your kids you love them **every day**, read the Bible together, pray *for* them, and pray *with* them. You will never regret it." (See Proverbs 22:6.)

AUNT VICKIE

Even though my parents did not provide my brother and me with a strong spiritual influence, God provided someone in our life who did. Her name was Vickie. Vickie was around from the time that my parents adopted Jerry until I was about nine years old. She was not a blood relative, but my brother and I both referred to her as Aunt Vickie. She was basically our nanny. When my mom and dad were working on an investment property, which was anytime they were not working at their full-time jobs, Vickie would take care of us. She and her elderly mother lived in one of my parent's rental homes.

Most of my happy memories as a child include Aunt Vickie. She was a constant source of encouragement in those early years, spending quality time with us and nurturing us, which we so desperately needed. She provided my brother and me what my parents could not. She took us to the beach, taught us how to cook, made crafts with us and even taught us sign language. The most important thing she did, however, was to repeatedly lay hands on Jerry and me and pray God's blessings over us. But I did not realize this until I was an adult. I believe those prayers are one of the reasons I am still alive today and serving God.

Unfortunately, the good times with Aunt Vickie didn't last. When I was nine, my parents felt it was necessary to move back to Iowa, believing the environment would be safer there than in

California and that we would have a better chance at getting a quality education.

The hardest thing about moving from California to Iowa was leaving Aunt Vickie. I will never forget the tears streaming down her face as we drove away. It was almost like I left a part of me in California. Sadly, it would be many years before I regained contact with her. Once we moved, life as I knew it drastically changed.

MEANWHILE, BACK ON THE FARM...

It was Father's Day 1976 when we moved back to the farm in Northwest Iowa where my mom grew up. Although we did not farm the land, we did have every kind of animal you could imagine. Once again my parents went to work for the school system—my dad for Northwestern College and my mom for the local high school. What a culture shock! We went from suburban Los Angeles to a farm in the Midwest that was five miles from the closest town. The weather was different, the people were different, the food was different—everything was different!

However, we were close to our family, which was a pleasant change I wasn't used to. It was nice being close to my relatives, especially my grandma on my mom's side. She was a wonderful Christian woman. She was the grandma that had the whole family over after church on Sundays for the noon meal. If I wasn't feeling well, her house was the house I went to after school. She knew how to knit, she traveled to really cool places on senior citizen's tours, and she always had treats! I really miss her sometimes. I wish she could be here to see how God has blessed me. Thankfully, I know I will see her again.

Living in the Midwest on a farm is where I learned to work hard. Most of my time was spent doing homework, housework and chores around the farm—including caring for all those animals. It wasn't long before I began to resent my parents. I felt like I was always working and never able to do anything fun. My friends eventually stopped asking if I could do things with them because the answer was always no. I guess it was my parents' way of protecting me.

In spite of my growing feelings of resentment toward my parents, I was basically a good kid. I never got into any trouble at school because my mom was always there watching me, and the same was true at home because she was the disciplinarian. My dad was very laid-back and never had much to say about anything. Sadly, I cannot remember a time in my childhood when I was not afraid of my mother. She was very strict and if you crossed her, it was not a good thing.

DEALING WITH SEVERE DISCIPLINE

Until the age of nine, spankings were a regular part of my life. There was a special place in our house for hanging the custom-made paddle. I don't remember how that paddle was broken, but I do remember it being replaced with a piece of what I now know to be PVC pipe. It was about eighteen to twenty-four inches long, and the marks it made were always cleverly concealed by clothing so that no one could detect them.

My brother, Jerry, always seemed to be able to escape spankings— at least I don't remember him getting as many as I did. It was not uncommon for him to run away from home. Unlike me, he was seemingly fearless. He was very independent and unaffected by my parents' fear tactics. One time, in an attempt to keep him from running away from a spanking, my mom threw the "stick" at him, but instead of hitting him, she hit and shattered the window in the back door of the house.

Needless to say, punishments at our house were usually severe. A roll of the eyes or a simple misunderstanding would result in a backhand that sent me to the floor. Anything that was perceived as backtalk from me resulted in a piece of soap being shoved in my mouth that I was expected to chew and swallow. Once, I remember spitting on the steps outside the backdoor, trying to get the soapy taste out of my mouth. My mom caught me and consequently made me scrub the steps with a scrub brush.

Once we moved to the farm in Iowa, lots of things changed— including the spankings. A horsewhip now replaced the piece of

PVC pipe, and if I tried to run, I was locked out of the house until my mom decided to let me in. Sometimes an entire day and night would pass before she allowed me back in the house, and then I still got whipped. As time passed, my resentment for her grew. I was embarrassed to show my legs because of the bruises and marks made by the horsewhip. When everyone else in my gym class was wearing shorts, I wore sweatpants so that the cuts wouldn't show. The older I got, the more I wished my mom would die so that I wouldn't be whipped anymore.

Severe discipline was such a big part of my life that it robbed me of any real happiness as a young teenager. There was really never any positive reinforcement—only criticism. I constantly tried to please my parents, especially my mom. I thought that if I could just behave and be good enough, I wouldn't get whipped. But this was impossible.

These types of incidents lasted until I was approximately sixteen. By that time, I couldn't wait to get out of the house. I wanted to get as far away from my parents as possible. Jerry left for the army the day after his high school graduation. He had dreamed of being a soldier all his life. With him gone, it was just my parents and me, which only made things worse. Without Jerry around for them to complain about, all their frustrations were taken out on me.

I vividly remember the last time my mom came after me with the whip. At that point in my life, I had become a very strong, muscular young girl—partly because of the hard physical labor around the farm, but also because I had lifted weights, training for track in junior high and high school.

In that moment when she was coming at me, something inside of me snapped. I grabbed the whip as she tried to hit me and yanked it out of her hands. I broke it into pieces and threw them back at her and said, "You will not do this to me anymore!" Enraged, she lunged to grab ahold of me, but I grabbed her around the neck first, trying my best to keep her from hurting me. At that point, my dad grabbed me and made me let her go. This was the only time I ever remember him intervening during one of these episodes. I felt so betrayed. All I could hear inside my head was, "What about me! What about what she is trying to do to me!"

The scuffle between my mom and me produced a large bruise around her neck, which she had a hard time explaining to everyone. I remember thinking, "Now you know how I feel." The good news is, she never hit me again.

Please understand that I believe there is a place for discipline in the home. However, it must be biblical—it must be administered in love, not anger, and done under the control of the Holy Spirit, not out of control. I do not agree with the way that I was disciplined as a child. Fear should never be used as a way to control someone. I learned personally that using fear to discipline breeds resentment and hostility toward parents. It also greatly hinders, if not destroying altogether, children's trust in their parents because they never really know what to expect from them. If a child cannot trust their own parents, who can they trust?

Today, both my mom and dad are with Jesus, and thankfully I don't hold any unforgiveness toward them. The truth is, they did not know or understand the ramifications of what they were doing. Had they known Jesus and had a relationship with Him like I do, they never would have raised us the way they did. Although it has taken many years, I have been healed from the emotional wounds inflicted upon me as a young person. The Holy Spirit is so gentle and kind. He has helped me deal with my feelings and put them under the blood of Jesus. I can sincerely say that I love my parents.

UNSPOKEN SHAME

In the midst of dealing with my parents' rigid and unrealistic expectations, the hard work around the farm, and their harsh discipline, my sexual identity was being formed. My earliest memory of sexual contact with a boy took place when I was around seven or eight years old. A male relative who was just a few years older than me used to take me downstairs in the basement of his house and "kiss" me. It didn't happen very often, and at the time it seemed innocent and harmless. Although I don't remember him ever hurting me, something just didn't feel right about it. Consequently, I did my best not to let anyone know about it.

The truth is, most of what I knew about boys I learned from magazines, books or television. With the exception of a movie that most kids see in fifth grade health class, I was never taught about "the birds and the bees." I do remember getting a copy of a children's book by Judy Blume that had very graphic scenes described in it. Ironically, my parents knew I had it, but they never took the time to look at it and find out if it was something I should be reading.

I was so afraid of my mom that I didn't dare do anything that would cause her to be mad at me. She was continually criticizing and cutting down the girls at school who were having sex, making them sound cheap and dirty, especially if they got pregnant. She always compared them to me and said the same thing would happen to me if I was allowed to go out like they were. I deeply resented that because I had never given them a reason not to trust me.

At the age of about eleven or twelve, I was introduced to pornography for the first time. While cleaning the house one day, I accidentally stumbled across an assortment of obscene magazines. I spent hours looking at them every week. Promiscuous thoughts about boys that I knew began to fill my head. But since my parents were so strict with me, I never had an opportunity to act out any of them.

I had no idea what I was opening myself up to by looking at those pornographic images. It was through those magazines that I learned about and began masturbating, which created a powerful prison that was seemingly inescapable. I remember praying, "God, if I ever masturbate again, I want You to kill me." I was so scared after I prayed that prayer… I knew masturbating was wrong, but I couldn't control it. I just knew God was going to kill me because I couldn't stop.

Added to this guilt and shame were the perverted encounters I had in my early teenage years with another male relative. On a regular basis, he gave me "lessons" on how to please a man. My thinking was so messed up by what I had seen in those magazines and I was so naïve that I just went along with whatever he wanted. In my heart, I knew what we were doing was wrong, but I was afraid to tell anyone.

All of these experiences severely twisted my view of relation-ships. I developed the mindset that the goal of every relationship between a man and a woman was sex, and with no one to tell me any differently, this is the way I entered my adult life.

It has been many years since I have thought about some of these things, and retelling them is very difficult. However, I believe it is necessary to reveal what happened so that you can understand why I made the choices I made once I left home as a young adult.

Chapter 2

THE GREAT ESCAPE

A Life of Freedom...or *Bondage?*

COLLEGE YEARS

Iwill never forget the day I went to college. I purposely chose a business school that had a new semester starting two weeks after I graduated from high school. It was just far enough from home that I would have to stay in the dorm. I was finally free from my parents.

The day I moved in, the college was still between semesters. There was virtually no one else in the dorm except one other girl. My parents dropped me off and left. I remember watching them drive away and thinking, *FREEDOM!!!*

I had never gotten drunk or smoked a cigarette until that afternoon. The one girl who was there came up to my room and introduced herself. She had a twelve pack of beer in one hand and cigarettes in the other. What a night that was! I had never been so sick in all my life, but I was partying! It didn't take me long to realize the party scene wasn't all it was cracked up to be. But everyone else was doing it, so I did too—just because I could.

I was so hungry for acceptance that I was willing to compromise just about anything to fit in and be "cool." I got drunk every weekend and quickly became a chain-smoker. I tried to hide it from my parents, but I know they knew. To keep from having to face them, I purposely got a job near the college so I wouldn't have to go home on weekends.

In a short time, I had my first boyfriend. I was only eighteen when we met, and I willingly gave up my virginity for him. I knew it was wrong, but because of the pornography I had been exposed to, my understanding of sex was extremely twisted. In my mind, I assumed I would have to marry him because we had gone "all the way." I had been taught not to have sex until marriage; therefore, the first person you have sex with you have to marry. It was the right thing to do.

Soon after, I started taking birth control pills. I didn't want to end up like one of the girls my mom used to talk about—a daughter who got pregnant and wasn't married, causing her family extreme embarrassment. I knew better then to ever go down that road. Ironically, even though I fiercely resented my parents, I still wanted to please them.

In the midst of my newfound college life, tragedy struck. On December 12, 1984, just a few months into my college career, one of the women I loved and admired most suddenly died. It was my grandma. She was the glue that held our family together on my mother's side. Once she was gone, things got really ugly. An awful spirit of greed took hold of many family members. I watched as they argued and fought about petty things. I witnessed lying, cheating and stealing of material possessions. It was sad and pitiful.

After Grandma's death, I began to party even more. Miraculously, I managed to graduate from college. With drinking and smoking still entrenched in my life, I chose to move to a town about ten miles from where I grew up. I secured a job working as a secretary at a local company. I was now engaged to my boyfriend, whom my parents didn't like, but that didn't matter to me. I was still convinced that I had to marry him. In my heart, I knew there had to be more to life than just partying every weekend. I had money, my own place, and my own car, but I was still not satisfied.

But then something unexpected happened; I met another man. He was a farmer who came from a wonderful Christian family. There was definitely something different about him—something special that attracted me to him. After breaking up with my boyfriend, he and I dated for five years, and everyone thought we were the perfect couple. I loved him more than anyone I had ever known—at least the way I understood love. Life with him would have probably been great, had I decided to stay.

But there was something inside of me that wasn't right—a driving feeling that I was being cheated out of experiencing everything life had to offer. There just had to be more excitement than what I had known living in a small farm town in Northwest Iowa. But what was it?

SAN DIEGO LIFE

It was the late 1980s, and by this time my brother, Jerry, was out of the army and living in San Diego. My parents had retired and were spending winters in California as well. In hopes of finding a better life, I decided to leave Iowa and move to San Diego and really start living.

I was so excited! San Diego, California! To my amazement, my parents loaned me $300 to make the drive from Iowa to California (our relationship had improved somewhat since I had moved out of the house). The trip was definitely interesting, to say the least. I was twenty-one years old, alone and driving halfway across the United States. Surprisingly, I wasn't scared at all. I was actually quite bold.

The first job I landed was at Gold's Gym. When that fizzled out, I got a job working at a title company downtown. Before long I discovered that the cost of living in San Diego was much higher than in Sioux Center, IA! The need for a second job became a stark realization. So to make ends meet, I began looking in the classified ads for a part-time job at night.

I found and applied for a job at a local bar working as a cocktail waitress. I must admit, I was surprised when I found out it was a *topless* bar. But since I wasn't going to be dancing, just waitressing, I quickly dismissed my fears and concerns.

The first few weeks were difficult, to say the least. I worked all day at the title company and then rushed home to change and work at the bar until 2:00 a.m. After about a month, I discovered that the dancers were making ten times as much money as I was—and I was working ten times harder. This eye-opening revelation infuriated me and moved me to action. I promptly went down to the Vice

Squad division at the San Diego Police Department and applied for my dancer's permit.

So now I was a dancer—a dancer known as Pepper. Amazingly, once I picked the name Pepper, no one called me Judy anymore— not even my brother. It was as if she had disappeared. Needless to say, the first time I got on stage I was pretty embarrassed, but I quickly got over it. Amazed at how much money I made that first night, I knew I was on to something. Almost overnight, I became one of the most popular dancers—sometimes making up to $1,000 a night. I thought I had it made! Consequently, I quit my job at the title company and began working at the bar full-time. I was now living in a house in La Jolla, California, with my brother and a friend of his. I was on cloud nine.

Until this time, I had never tried any kind of drugs. I only drank occasionally and smoked cigarettes. After awhile, though, I began to notice how thin the other dancers were and I wondered how they stayed that way. One girl told me her secret was prescription diuretics. She had gotten them from her doctor simply by telling him she was bloated all the time. Since the diuretics helped her stay skinny, I thought I would give it a try. After all, it wasn't like smoking marijuana. This was legal and all I had to do to get it was tell a little "white lie."

Well, for awhile they worked. But I still wasn't as thin as the other dancers. I didn't want to be too thin; however, I was very competitive, and I wanted to be the best. I knew that most of the girls smoked marijuana and used cocaine. What I didn't know was that most of them were also using a very popular methamphetamine called crystal meth. It is a cocaine substitute that is just as powerful but cheaper. Once I discovered that this was the "magic trick" most of the dancers were using to keep themselves thin, I bought in to the "notion of the potion."

At first, I really didn't like the idea of taking crystal meth. I had always looked down on drug addicts, and I didn't want to end up looking like one of the strung-out, lifeless people you see on TV or read about in the news. Somehow, though, I didn't see myself that way. *After all*, I thought, *I'm not going to overdose or anything. I'm just using enough to curb my appetite. I love the way it makes my eyes look—pretty pupils that are dazzlingly dilated all the time.*

At that point in my life, I smoked about a pack of cigarettes a day, but if you were to ask me if I was a smoker, I would quickly tell you no. I just didn't like to be labeled. I had convinced myself that I could quit smoking anytime, and the same thing was true about taking crystal meth. I felt like I could maintain control of what I took, and that I would never end up hooked. It simply couldn't happen—not to me anyway. Right?

Wrong. As you might have guessed, I quickly became addicted to crystal meth—so much so that I always had to have it. As a result, I became so thin that I looked deathly sick. And yet, in my mind, I was still convinced that I could quit whenever I wanted. I just didn't want to yet. Besides, all the drug dealers wanted to hang out with me because I could introduce them to the other dancers. On the surface it seemed like the perfect set-up: I had all the money, men and drugs I wanted.

But I had a big problem—I didn't trust anybody. And the crystal meth only made matters worse by adding to my paranoia. I hardly ever ate or slept. I lived life believing that people, especially men, only hung out with me to use me for my connections. So every chance I got, I took full advantage of it and was able to get seemingly anything I wanted. Sometimes when I got too much meth in my system at one time, I would hallucinate. Once, I remember getting some bad stuff and hallucinating so horribly that I was convinced all the hairs on my body were worms that were alive and crawling all over me. Times like these really freaked me out.

Another problem I had was pride—I became so overly confident in myself that I thought I was invincible. I had a filthy mouth, and anyone who crossed me definitely got a taste of it. I wasn't afraid of anything or anybody. I dated anyone I wanted, and when I was through with him, I moved on to my next "challenge." I particularly liked to get the guy that no one else could get. It was a kind of game I played.

I remember one particular guy who came into the bar one night and immediately caught my eye. He was obviously a body builder and extremely handsome. While all the girls were trying to get his attention, I decided to play hard-to-get. Eventually, his friend came up to me and said, "What color are your eyes?" I gave him some smart response initially but finally told him they were green. As it turned out, I was just the "type" of girl his striking friend was looking for. The result: another meaningless, unfulfilling relationship totally based on lust.

With this kind of twisted thinking and behavior, you can see how I quickly made quite a number of enemies, especially among the other dancers. No longer was I the sweet, innocent "girl next door" type. I had changed. My attitude had changed. My goals had changed. Everything about me had changed. But I was the only one who couldn't see it. People tried to tell me that the changes in me weren't good, but I didn't listen. Instead, I cussed them out and told them they were jealous of my success.

Slowly but surely, my world began to crumble all around me, and I didn't even recognize it. I was so consumed with *me* that I couldn't see the direction in which I was going. I had hooked up with all the wrong people, and my life was beginning to spiral downward rapidly.

I had people thrown out of the bar all the time. If someone looked at me the wrong way, I told the bouncers, and they would throw them out. One night I had a guy who was once a friend of mine thrown out of the bar just because I didn't like him anymore and didn't feel like looking at him that night. Angrily, he threatened me, telling me I had made a very serious mistake. I blew off his threats and laughed at him while the bouncers threw him out.

What I didn't know, however, was that he was working for a drug dealer that I hated, and he had more power and influence than I did. At the time, I was dating the general manager of the bar, and it just so happened that he owed this particular drug dealer quite a bit of money. So to get even with me, they threatened him, saying if he didn't fire me, they would tell the owners of the bar.

He had no choice but to fire me. After all, he was a "family man" with a wife and kids to support. So in one afternoon, my whole life came crashing down around me. No more dancing, which meant no more money, which meant no more drugs. I was furious, but powerless to do anything about it.

Overwhelmed and stunned by the situation, I was beside myself wondering what to do. In an instant, I got a bright idea to take a trip to Las Vegas. I thought, *What's the harm? It might be fun. I need a break anyway. I haven't been to Las Vegas since I was a kid, and I need to get away from San Diego.* A bouncer friend of mine named Billy and a few of his friends thought the idea was great. So we packed into a pickup truck and headed to Vegas.

Looking back, I have learned that you can justify anything, if you want to do it bad enough. When I was a cocktail waitress, I said I would never be a dancer. When I was a dancer, I said I would never do drugs. When I did drugs, I said I wasn't an addict. When I was an addict, I said I would never stoop to dating a drug dealer or hanging out with them just to support my habit. Amazingly, **all** the things I said I would *never* do, I had done—except one.

P. 54

LAS VEGAS

Living life in the fast lane, my friends and I headed out on what was supposed to be a weeklong trip to Las Vegas. The five-hour drive out there was awesome. Of course, once we arrived, we "painted the town red" and partied. But after a few nights, the money ran out and so did the meth. With my world in San Diego now shattered, a new life in Vegas seemed to pack great potential.

A vote was taken, and the decision was unanimous. We drove back to San Diego, got our things, and made the trip back to Vegas to start new lives. The guys started selling perfume door-to-door, and I went to work in one of the local topless bars. It wasn't long before things really started happening. I thought I hit it big when I met a guy who said he had lots of connections with people who had meth. Needless to say, we began partying with him on a regular basis.

One night, he told us that some wealthy friends of his were coming in from out of town, and they wanted to party with us. Well, since I was always up for a good time and still not afraid of anything, I said sure.

As promised, his wealthy out-of-town friends arrived and in style. Pulling up in a luxurious limousine, they told my female friends and me that they were taking us to a party house that was about an hour outside of town. Excitedly, we all got in and headed for what we thought would be the time of our lives. After driving for what seemed like much longer than an hour, we finally arrived at our destination. The moment I stepped out of the limo, I knew something wasn't right. For one, there were no other cars at the house, and secondly, we were out in the middle of the desert.

When they took us inside, we met the "owner" of the house. At that point, it was clear that we were not there for a party. The house we had been brought to was a brothel—a house of prostitution. Instantly, I was enraged at the people who brought us out there and demanded they take me back. "I'm not into hookers!" I shouted.

Remember the one thing I hadn't done that I said I would never do? This was it. I hated hookers. I used to make fun of them when I came out of the bar after it closed each night. I thought being a topless dancer was so much better than what they were doing. The guys in the bar would watch us dance and then go to them afterward to get what they couldn't get from us. In my mind, hookers were an embarrassment to women. I looked at them and thought, *They are so cheap. I would never sell myself like that.* This is the fury that fueled my protest.

Seeing how upset I was, the owner started talking to me, trying to calm me down. He was very interested in keeping me there and told me everything he could think of to sway me to stay. "You don't have to do anything you don't want to do," he said. But the thing that really caught my attention was when he told me how much money I could make working there. Wow! Within moments, I warmed up to the idea and began to change my attitude. I agreed to stay for a week or two, thinking to myself, *What do I have to lose?*

In a short amount of time, I learned how to manipulate the system the owner had set up for his "house." Every "John" that came in the door had the choice of which lady he wanted. Since the other ladies in the house were a lot older, I was always chosen over them. Before long, I was making more money than I had ever made in my life! Although I was supposed to give half of everything I made each night to the owner, I never did. He was never in the house, so he didn't know how much I was making. He and his wife lived in a trailer behind the brothel, where he spent most of his time. I also hid my stash of meth, and he never even suspected I had it.

I quickly became the owner's top moneymaker, and to keep me happy, he allowed me to take trips into Vegas every once in a while to go shopping. He even hired a driver to take me back and forth. I stayed at the really cool casinos and just hung out by myself. When I was ready to go back, I simply made a phone call, and the driver picked me up. What a life! I thought I had everything a girl could ever want. Until one day when something unexpected happened again.

Chapter 3

IN TRANSITION

Meeting Mr. Right

NO CHOICE IN THE MATTER

I noticed it had been over month since my last period. I had a very regular cycle, so I was concerned. To know for sure if my gut feeling was right, I bought an over-the-counter pregnancy test. Sure enough, it was positive. *Great!* I thought. *Now what am I going to do?* Being pregnant is not good for business when you are a prostitute. *Maybe the test was wrong*, I thought. So I got another one, and it was positive, too. Now it was clear. I had a problem on my hands that I could not just "fix" like I was accustomed to doing.

I had to tell the owner and his wife. To my amazement, they weren't surprised. As a matter of fact, his wife said, "No problem. We'll take care of it. Tomorrow I'll drive you into town and we'll get rid of this little problem." Her plan was to drive me into town for an appointment at an abortion clinic—a trip she had apparently made before.

I cannot accurately describe my feelings as I lay awake all night thinking about what was going to happen. I knew in my heart abortion was wrong. Until this point, I had prided myself on only having broken nine of the Ten Commandments. There was one that I knew I could never break: "Thou shalt not murder." But having an abortion would end my so-called "bragging rights." As I lay there trying to go to sleep and wondering who the father might be, I remember talking to God and asking Him to forgive me. I also remember talking to the baby and asking him to forgive me too. I knew it was wrong, but I felt like I was trapped and had no choice.

The time came and went, and the procedure was done. The whole thing took less than a day. The doctor told me I was supposed to rest and remain flat on my back for two weeks, but I was up working that night.

Several days passed. It seemed to be business as usual, until late one night when a certain customer called on us. All the other ladies were sleeping when the bell rang. Since it was my turn to welcome the arrivals, I went out to let in the new John. *Wow! This guy is big*, I thought. *Oh well, just another routine sucker that I can take advantage of.* But I was wrong.

NOT YOUR ORDINARY "JOHN"

I knew right away that there was something different about this guy. He was very innocent and seemingly vulnerable. It became apparent rather quickly that he had never done anything like this before. Seeing he was very nervous, I tried to make him feel at ease with some casual conversation. His name was Rick, and this was his first time to Las Vegas. He had been married for eight years, but he and his wife had recently split up.

For years, Rick felt like he was living the American Dream. He had a wife, two daughters, a nice home and a thriving real estate business. Life was good until shortly before Christmas 1990. At that point, life as he knew it came crashing down. His wife told him that they needed to separate, and then he discovered she was involved in an adulterous relationship with a close family friend. Conditions at home became so bad that he had no choice but to move out of the house.

Feeling empty inside, Rick started looking for something to fill the void. He started drinking and smoking, which he hadn't done for years. He was desperately searching for something to remove the pain of rejection. He threw himself even more into his work, laboring an average of sixteen hours a day. The rest of his time was mainly spent drinking, with a little bit of sleep thrown in.

Long before his marriage blew up, he had made plans to attend a real estate conference in Las Vegas. Unfortunately, he hadn't reserved a room, and all the rooms were booked due to other conventions in town. While looking for a vacancy, he overheard someone asking for directions to the brothels. This piqued his interest, and in his tired and tattered frame of mind, he got into his car and drove out to the brothels, stopping at the first one he came to.

Ironically, when I told Rick my name was Judy, he responded, "Great, I am trying to get rid of a wife named Judy." He didn't care much about women and was not looking for any kind of a relationship—other than the kind we were about to have.

While he was speaking, part of me began to think about how I was going to spend all the money I made off of him. I thought, *All I have to do is listen to his sob story and convince him that I actually care, and he'll buy it—hook, line and sinker.* But for some reason, I didn't have the heart to do it.

I could see how deeply he had been hurt, and for the first time something was awakened inside of me that had been dormant for a long time—compassion. I actually felt sympathy for him and wanted to help him in some way. He didn't need a prostitute; he needed a friend...someone he could trust. I didn't know why, but I really wanted to be that person.

We talked for quite awhile before he left. Because it was so late and he was so tired, I was concerned that he would not be able to make the hour-long drive back to Las Vegas. So I gave him directions to a little casino motel just up the road. I watched him as he gathered his things and then drove away.

For some reason my emotions were awakened, and I didn't know how to handle them. I actually cared about this guy. Out of concern for his safety, I called the motel I had directed him to. They put me through to his room. After the phone rang several times and I was just about ready to hang up, he answered. I told him I just wanted to make sure he made it there safely. He was surprised to hear from me and encouraged by my call.

We talked for awhile longer, and he asked if he could call me again. I said sure and gave him my number. After we hung up, I felt so excited but didn't know why. All I could think about the next day was this guy. Would he call? Would I ever hear from him again? Part of me really hoped I would, and part of me was thinking, *Get real*.

THE ATTRACTION GROWS

Well, I did hear from him again. He called me when he got back to Vegas and asked if I would join him for dinner while he was still in town. When I asked my boss about it, he said no way.

Rick was only going to be in Vegas for a few days during a convention, and then he would be going back home to Lancaster, Pennsylvania. After my boss told me I couldn't go into town for dinner, I thought I would never see or hear from Rick again. But much to my surprise, that was not the case. The next day he called, and we talked for hours. He told me he would like for me to visit him in Pennsylvania. Laughing, I responded, "If my boss wouldn't let me go into town to have dinner with you, he definitely won't let me fly to Pennsylvania!"

For several weeks, Rick and I had extended conversations, talking about everything under the sun. Again, he asked me to come and visit him. Rick made Pennsylvania sound so wonderful. He described the changes of the seasons and the Amish people that lived nearby. His descriptions reminded me of the small town in Iowa where I grew up and how simple my life seemed to be when I lived there. No alcohol, no cigarettes, no drugs, no prostitution and no stress. It sounded so inviting.

Something inside of me desperately wanted to go, but I knew my boss wouldn't let me. Day by day, my tolerance of the Vegas lifestyle was weakening and I grew more and more disgusted with myself. Regretfully, I had become the very thing I hated.

One day after another long phone conversation with Rick, I boldly went to my boss and said, "If you don't let me go to Pennsylvania, I will leave here and never come back!" I really had no clue how he would respond. But for some reason, he agreed to let me go. I gave him my word that I would come back. He looked at me and said, "I hope you know what you're doing."

Excitedly, I called Rick and said, "Buy me a plane ticket to

Pennsylvania and I'm there!" Without hesitation, he sent the ticket Federal Express and in a matter of days, I was off to Lancaster, Pennsylvania.

A TASTE OF A BETTER LIFE

Rick met me at the airport with roses! I was overwhelmed. Unfortunately, I was still snorting and smoking meth every day. It was actually a miracle that I wasn't arrested at the airport with all the drugs I had in my possession.

Once I was with Rick, I was able to relax and enjoy myself. We went bowling, ate ice cream, and played pool. (I was actually quite the pool shark from my days in the bar.) While there, I had the opportunity to meet his daughters and see how they genuinely adored their daddy. Truly, it was the most refreshing three days I had experienced in such a long time.

When it came time for me to return to Vegas, I didn't want to go and Rick didn't want me to leave. But not knowing exactly what my boss would do, I didn't want to take a chance on not going back. Deeply distraught, I managed to get on the plane. It was one of the hardest things I have ever had to do. I was crying and Rick was crying. But inside I just knew I would see him again. I didn't know how, and I didn't know when; but I knew deep inside that I would see him again.

When I got back to the brothel, my boss was actually surprised to see me. I glared at him and said, "I gave you my word that I would return, and I have kept it." The next few days were awful. I hated every moment. I hated the house, the other girls, my boss and my life. I just had to get out. I knew that if I stayed there, I would probably overdose, be murdered or die from some sexually transmitted disease.

Finally, when I could take it no more, I packed what I could fit into a suitcase and gave everything else to the other girls. I went to my boss, looked him straight in the eye and said, "I'm leaving and I'm not coming back. I just can't do this anymore." Somehow he must have known I wouldn't be useful to him anymore, so he let me go.

I called Rick and said, "If you will have me, I want to come to Pennsylvania and be with you." To my surprise, he replied, "I was going to call you today and tell you to come back because I want you to be with me." His words were music to my ears! They couldn't have been more perfect. I promptly purchased a one-way plane ticket, called my friend (who was also my dealer) and told her to come and get me.

She quickly drove me to the airport. When we arrived, I got out and handed her my last bag of crystal meth. I told her, "Take this. I won't be needing it anymore." She laughed at me in disbelief and took the bag. I turned my back and walked into the airport. At that moment, God supernaturally delivered me from my debilitating drug addiction without going through rehab. Pepper was dying…Judy was coming back to life.

Chapter 4

A BRAND-NEW START
Rediscovering Life and Meaningful Living

REUNITED AND IT FEELS SO GOOD

My mind was in overdrive trying to imagine what my new life with Rick was going to be like. Countless questions raced through my head, like, *What if this doesn't work? What am I getting myself into? What if he changes his mind and wants to get back together with his wife?* And *Will I be satisfied with one guy the rest of my life?* For years, all I had known was drugs, bars, prostitution and more meaningless relationships than I cared to remember. Somehow, though, in spite of all my apprehensions and fears, I knew that we were meant to be together and everything was going to be all right.

When Rick met me at the airport this time, it was as if we had been together for years. We picked up right where we had left off and got to know each other more and more over the next two months. It was amazing. Although I slept more in the first four weeks we were together than I had in previous months, he didn't seem to mind. He knew I had been through a lot and was willing to help me in whatever way he could to see me totally free.

Almost instinctively, I made a decision to begin going to church again, and Rick was in full agreement. In fact, he had already started going to church after he returned from Vegas. It was a Presbyterian church that was filled with some of the nicest people you would ever want to meet. Rick had met and become friends with the associate pastor through attending some of the events for singles, so we decided to make that our church home.

Before long, I began to attend their women's Bible study. I was hungry to learn about God. I always loved God and had had a place for Him in my heart since childhood. But apart from the brief time my brother and I had with Aunt Vickie, I lacked the ongoing instruction of His Word and the true example of His unconditional love. Realizing that there was so much to learn, I purchased the Bible on cassette and began to listen to it every day.

Since Rick was in the process of finalizing his divorce when we reunited, we needed to wait awhile before we could get married. In the meantime, we made wedding plans and set the date for July 28, 1991—the day after his divorce was final.

The wedding was very small and quaint, with just close family members attending. My parents were there along with Aunt Vickie, and the pastor that Rick had met at the single's event married us. He and Rick played racquetball together quite often, and we actually became good friends with him and his family.

PRESSING FOR PERFECTION

Time passed and I enjoyed married life more than I could have imagined. It felt good living a clean life, free of the nagging fear of possibly getting caught for doing something illegal. Although we both had baggage that we brought into our relationship, we were determined to make our marriage work. Oh, we had occasional moments of "intense fellowship," but we always made it through.

I never regretted leaving Las Vegas for one moment. I knew I had made the right decision to move to Pennsylvania and marry Rick. I was determined to become the perfect housewife.

Interestingly, of all the changes and adjustments I had made up to that point, nothing scared me more than cooking. But by God's grace, we managed to eat okay. During our first year of marriage, I lived by a cookbook we received as a wedding gift. Rick was always such a good sport. Although he never knew what to expect for dinner each night, he never complained. Even when I made tater-tot casserole and the hamburger was raw, he just politely suggested that we should wait awhile before having that meal again.

Not many people knew about our past—not even our parents. We felt that they simply wouldn't understand. Rick and I didn't see any reason to reveal all the skeletons in our closet to everyone. He had a prosperous real estate career, and if people knew how we met, it might jeopardize his business.

Our parents, however, did know about the abortion, and my dad in particular, had a hard time accepting it. Over and over again, he made critical comments about the situation. He just couldn't forgive me, and he let me know that as often as he could. Although his words hurt me deeply, I didn't show it.

All my life, I held tightly to the hope of someday getting his approval. Sadly, this one thing that I wanted and needed so desperately I would never get. Although my mom told me of times when my dad talked about how proud he was of me, he never uttered those words to me personally.

POSITIVELY PREGNANT

Just nine days before our wedding, Rick and I were surprised to discover that we were going to have a baby. The home test was positive, and so was the one at the doctor's office. I was pregnant and the baby was due in the spring. My life was changing so fast it was hard to keep up.

During the weeks and months leading up to the delivery, I was able to stay at home, which was a huge blessing. I continued to listen to the Bible on cassette every day and study Scripture whenever I had the chance. I also learned how to cross-stitch and knit, which enabled me to begin making baby blankets. I even made latch hook rugs!

Without question, I loved being pregnant. I started wearing maternity clothes the day after we found out. Words can't describe the feelings I had the first time I felt the baby move. What a wonderful experience!

One thing I had to temporarily get used to was not being able to see my feet. I had never experienced that before. I still remember looking in the mirror and thinking, *Will I ever look the same again?*

This was especially true during the third trimester when the stretch marks began to appear.

There was one thing, however, that was not so wonderful: the overwhelming thoughts of condemnation and guilt that seemed to come out of nowhere. It was a spiritual battle, but at the time, I was totally unaware of it.

Every so often, Rick came home and found me sitting on the sofa sobbing uncontrollably. For awhile, I couldn't describe what was wrong. But eventually, I came to realize that I was feeling guilty for being pregnant. Again and again, I heard a voice in my mind saying, *You don't deserve to have a baby because you had an abortion. This baby will not live, and if by chance it does, it will be horribly deformed.*

Needless to say, I was terrified. I didn't know what to do. I thought I was going crazy. I prayed and repeatedly repented for the abortion, but the memory of it hung over my head like a dark cloud.

What made matters worse was that the women's Bible study I was attending at the time had been debating the subject of abortion, and many were mercilessly criticizing women who had elected to have one. The critical comments they were making about women in that situation were so painful for me to listen to; they were so one-sided. Ironically, no one there knew about my past.

At one point when I could take their comments no longer, I stood up and boldly rebuked them for their pious attitudes. I revealed to them the fact that I had had an abortion and shared how much I wished I could change that decision now. I also spoke about the guilt, condemnation, shame and torment I was dealing with as a result. I told them that they shouldn't sit and judge those who've had an abortion, but rather pray for them, because they don't know the whole story behind why someone chose that option.

When I finished speaking, you could have heard a pin drop and there wasn't a dry eye in the place. They had never thought about it from that perspective before.

Thankfully, I was able to find some relief through post-abortion counseling offered through a crisis pregnancy center. I even ended up volunteering for them, talking to people on their crisis hotline. Still, I couldn't totally break free from the guilt and shame I felt.

WELCOME TO MOTHERHOOD!

Finally, it was time for the baby to be born. Due to some unexpected complications, I ended up having an emergency C-section. Nevertheless, on March 21, 1992, I gave birth to the most beautiful girl in the world. To me, she was perfect. I had no idea what to do with her, but she was perfect! Never in my life had I known love for anyone like I loved that little baby. We named her Victoria Ruth, after my Aunt Vickie and my mother.

Within days I realized just how little I knew about parenting. Diapering, nursing, burping and crying became my life. Three weeks after she was born, I asked Rick if we could take her back. I felt so overwhelmed and inadequate; I just didn't feel I was cut out to be a parent. But in his gentle way, he assured me that we would make it, and we did.

Unfortunately, after Victoria's birth I still struggled with many of the same fearful thoughts as before. I was filled with an over-whelming sense that something was going to happen to my baby. I began to think that if I could do something to make up for the abortion, everything would be okay. But nothing I ever did seemed to be good enough. It was an endless tormenting cycle.

Then I thought, *Perhaps if I care for children that are less fortunate, maybe that will make amends for my former sins.* So Rick and I became foster parents, trying to act on our limited understanding of James 1:27. However, that was a big mistake because God was not in it. Since we didn't have His *blessing* to be foster parents, we didn't have His *power* to be foster parents.

Originally, what I really wanted to do was care for special needs babies, but the foster care agency would only give us teenagers who had been in trouble with the law. We had absolutely no idea how to care for youth from this type of background, and it was obvious. To make matters worse, I became overly concerned about what people thought of us; I wanted others to see us as "spiritual." But we just ended up miserable.

Indeed, it was a hard lesson to learn, but a very important one. God made it very clear to Rick and me that He only expects us to do what He asks us to do. And whatever God asks us to do, He will give us the power and skill to do. Anything that constantly frustrates us, drains us and steals our joy is probably not of Him.

A TEST OF FAITH

When our daughter, Victoria, was about twelve months old, Rick and I decided we wanted to have another baby. I wanted the kids to be close in age, and Rick didn't want Victoria to be an only child. Since he already had two daughters from his previous marriage and we had our little girl, I really wanted to give him a boy. Especially because I knew that we would not be having any other children after this.

For about one month, we tried to get pregnant and nothing happened. It was hard for me to begin to imagine the emotional turmoil that couples who try to get pregnant for years and are unsuccessful go through. I was devastated after only *one* month.

In the women's Bible study I was attending at that time, we were studying the story of Hannah, learning how she fasted and prayed and asked the Lord to give her a son. She promised God that if He would answer her prayer, she would give her son back to the Lord to serve Him all the days of his life. I thought to myself, *If God did that for Hannah, I'll bet He'll do it for me.*

I made up my mind to fast every Tuesday for one month. I don't know why I picked Tuesday, but I did. At the time, I had never fasted before and I didn't know anything about it. However, I believed that if it worked for Hannah, it would work for me. Sure enough, not long after I started fasting, I got pregnant! Of course, I would have to wait a few months before I could find out if God had fully answered my prayer. But I trusted He would come through.

GOD DELIVERS ON A PROMISE

Almost overnight, I began to look pregnant. I got so big so fast that the midwife I was seeing for prenatal care wanted me to have a sonogram done to see if I was carrying more than one baby. She said, "The last time I saw someone get that big that fast, she had quintuplets!" Her comment did not excite me.

Well, by the time the sonogram was done, I was far enough along to determine the sex of the baby. I was so excited! I didn't even care about having to drink the two liters of liquid required before the test. (For those of you who have been pregnant, you probably know what I'm talking about!)

As I lay on the table about to explode, the attendant determined that there was just one big baby in my belly. Needless to say, I was relieved. But when she had a rather surprised look on her face, I asked her what was wrong. With a partial smile, she replied, "Do you want to know the sex of your baby?"

I looked at Rick and said, "Well, are you ready?" When he said yes, she turned the monitor around so that we could see the baby. The moment she pointed to the tiny appendage between the baby's legs, I nearly leaped off the table. My prayer was answered! Right there, I began to praise God for His goodness. When I glanced over at Rick again, he had giant tears rolling down his cheeks. He was speechless. God had honored my childlike faith, and I was amazed.

That night, I took a few minutes to journal what had taken place. I wrote, "PRAISE THE LORD! WE ARE HAVING A SON! The joy that fills my heart knows no bounds today! Lord, You are so gracious! I LOVE YOU, LORD! Thanks be to God! He has answered my prayer!"

Gratefully, the second pregnancy was as wonderful as the first. But when they said the baby was big, they weren't kidding. The day he was born, he weighed nearly ten pounds. The nurse took one look at him and said, "My goodness! Look at the size of his hands and feet!" She made it sound like I had given birth to a Great Dane or something. And he cried so loud that he woke up all the babies in the nursery! Oh! But he was precious, and he was mine.

We decided to name him after the three most important men in our lives. Christian (after Jesus Christ), Lawrence (after Rick's dad who went home to be with the Lord two months prior to Christian's birth), and Vanderham (after my dad).

Knowing that this would be my last pregnancy, I greatly desired to have him naturally. But because he was so big and I was so small, it was not an option. Nevertheless, God had given me a son. And I purposed in my heart to keep my commitment to dedicate Him to the Lord. I was so happy.

Chapter 5

FACING NEW CHALLENGES
Growing Pains and the Dangers of Compromise

SORTING THROUGH THE LUGGAGE

As with any marriage, there are always new challenges to face as a husband and wife grow together, and ours was no exception. Suffice it to say our marriage was anything but smooth sailing. We both brought baggage and wounds into our relationship, and some were more severe than others.

While Rick's biggest issue was overcoming the rejection he had received from his previous wife, mine was an unwillingness to be intimate. Coming out of the lifestyle of prostitution made it very difficult for me to see sex in any other way than negative.

For many years I hated men and had a very poor opinion of them. I had been deeply hurt by the men in my life, especially those close to me. As a result, I was fiercely determined not to let anyone ever get too close to me or take advantage of me again.

Prior to meeting Rick, I believed that men only wanted one thing from me—sex. Unfortunately, I was convinced that he had married me for the same reason. I thought, *Why else would a man marry a prostitute if it wasn't because he wanted to have sex all the time?* This twisted thinking was the reason I became a prostitute in the first place. My attitude was, *If that's what men want, why shouldn't I capitalize on it and use it to my advantage?*

With this kind of thinking ingrained in my mind, I was unable to totally give myself to Rick as a wife should. Out of fear, I operated under the assumption that if I didn't open myself up to others, I wouldn't get hurt again. I vowed to never again give in to the sexual desires and demands of others. Unfortunately, when I said no to sex, Rick felt rejected all over again.

I came up with every excuse I could think of to not have sex—even on our wedding night. My view was so tainted that I convinced myself that sex was wrong and God was not pleased with it. I also believed that if sex was the only reason Rick married me, I would teach him that nobody could use me and get away with it. Little did I know that I was missing out on one of the best parts of what God intended for a husband and wife.

PLACING THE BLAME

As time passed, the tension between Rick and me continued to intensify. Ironically, I was convinced that most of the problems we were facing were his fault. It was easy for me to point the finger of blame at him. Then I didn't have to look at the problems in my own life. I was often quick to point out his flaws and failures. I would say I was a nag, but that really doesn't fully express how I tried to bully him into submission.

Before I met Rick, I always imagined that I would marry someone like one of the bodybuilders I met in the bar. The truth is, though, the relationships I had with men like that meant very little to me and never lasted. They were only "skin deep." So even though Rick was not the ideal "type" of man I *wanted*, I eventually realized he was the type of man I *needed*. He had many wonderful qualities a godly man should have. I was just too blind to see them.

Again and again, I tried to "fix" him. I'd say things like, "If you would just pray and read the Bible more, things around here would be different," or "If you would just fellowship with other godly men more, then you would grow up enough and be able to love me like Christ loves the church." And while I ranted and raved, he just sat there quietly and listened to me pridefully preach at him. As much as I badgered him, it is truly a miracle that he stuck with me.

DISCOVERING THE ROOT OF MY PROBLEM

By God's grace, I came to recognize that the root of my problem was centered in my inability to trust others. Because I had been abused, neglected and taken advantage of, I had a very hard time trusting anybody, including Rick. Please understand that I really loved him and knew in my heart that he was the man for me. But I still had a hard time believing he really loved me and didn't have any hidden motives.

My inability to truly trust affected every area of our relationship. We argued about everything from sex and money, to the kids and a clean house. Interestingly, no one ever knew. Everyone thought we were the perfect couple. But behind the scenes, I was following the example I grew up with. For years I watched my mom "wear the pants" in the family, so I thought I should do the same thing. I had no knowledge of the principle of submission to authority. Consequently, I rebelled against it—especially male authority.

Remember, as Pepper the dancer, I was bold, brazen, mouthy and driven. To me, submission was a sign of weakness, which totally went against my character. To submit to Rick or anyone else in authority would make me vulnerable, and my fear and pride would not let me go there. The few times I did allow myself to be vulnerable and trust someone, they broke my heart. I wasn't about to go through that kind of pain again.

Rick and I also struggled with issues regarding his ex-wife and his other two children. Out of deep insecurity, I began to resent the other children because they took his attention away from me, Victoria, and Christian. On top of that, we had to pay child support. It seemed as though his other children had everything, while we went without. And that just didn't seem fair. What made this situation even worse is that during the first few years we were married, they lived only a few blocks away.

In desperation, I began to cry out to the Lord even more. Day after day, I prayed and asked Him to help me change. I desperately wanted to be a wonderful Christian wife and completely give myself to Rick. In His mercy, the Lord began to show me that I needed to seek Him so He could begin to fix me. He also showed me that if I would get out of the way and leave Rick alone, He would begin to deal with him. It was not my job to fix Rick; it was God's.

ONE STEP FORWARD

Once I began to see how many problems I had, I purposed in my heart to seek God daily. I had problems with pride, selfishness, greed, lack of integrity, lack of excellence and a host of other things. At that time, I was still at home with both of my kids, so every day when they took their nap, I prayed and studied the Bible. On average, I spent three to four hours in the Word and in prayer. I even wrote out the Gospels so that I could remember them, and I was still listening to the Bible on cassette every day. I was so hungry to know the Word of God, and studying the Scripture fascinated me. Looking back, I am so thankful for that season in my life. I believe that the foundation of my relationship with the Lord was built during that time. Although I didn't see immediate change, gradually things did begin to improve.

I got to a point, however, where my walk with God reached a plateau. I couldn't seem to grow any further. I had begun to experience a certain level of victory in many areas of my life, but something was missing. I couldn't quite put my finger on it, but I knew there must be more to being a Christian than what I was experiencing. I still did not have total victory over guilt and condemnation or those fearful thoughts that were coming against my mind. Likewise, my attitude still needed to be adjusted, and I still didn't have complete control of the harsh words coming out of my mouth. I needed something to push me over into victory, but I didn't know what it was.

This went on for a few years. Things went well for quite some time, and the overall quality of our lives improved dramatically. Rick and I became active in our church, and his real estate business began to really take off. At that point, the kids were a little older, so I decided to join Rick and start working with him at his office. Once I secured my real estate license and enrolled the kids into daycare, we began working non-stop.

TWO STEPS BACK

Unfortunately, it was at this point that we also began to gradually slide back into our old lifestyle of partying. Little by little, I slacked off of spending time with God, and our church attendance began to drop off. We began to party on the weekends again and skip church. Initially, it seemed like harmless fun. *We're not really hurting anyone*, we thought.

Once again, however, we began to struggle with a lot of the same issues in our marriage. For awhile we just seemed to glide over them unaffected. No one suspected we were having problems because we put on such a good front. The real estate field was filled with adulterous affairs, a lack of integrity, greed and selfishness. But Rick and I weren't participating in any of that, so we thought we were ok.

Then one weekend while partying at a friend's house, things really got out of hand. Rick and I both had way too much to drink, and we got into a terrible fight over, you guessed it, sex. Rick wanted it, and I didn't want to give it to him. For Rick, it was the straw that broke the camel's back. At that point we both came to the conclusion that our relationship just wasn't working and we should probably go our separate ways.

For several weeks we considered separating, until a lady that we worked with in the real estate office talked to us. Her name was Norma, and she was one of the sweetest ladies I'd ever known. She was a Christian woman who was definitely different. She always said things like, "Praise the Lord," and "in Jesus' Name." With a discerning heart, Norma noticed the direction Rick and I were headed. One day she invited us to a weekly Bible study at her house. Not wanting to hurt her feelings and trying to overcome the feelings of guilt for all the partying we had been doing, we accepted. Neither Rick nor I had any idea what was about to happen.

Chapter 6

A NEW DIMENSION
OF GOD'S POWER

Submerged in the Holy Spirit

THE BIBLE STUDY

For some reason, I was nervous about going to this Bible study. I don't know if it was conviction about all the partying we had been doing or just the result of the sad condition of our marriage. Whatever the case, we got the children packed into the car and headed out.

When we arrived, everything seemed to be going just fine. There was nothing out of the ordinary taking place, which was the way I had hoped it would be. The topic being discussed that night was the baptism of the Holy Spirit, a subject I was somewhat familiar with. I had been studying the Bible for quite some time, and I was very familiar with Acts 2. However, something was different. The teacher didn't just present the story as a matter of history; she made it sound like the baptism of the Holy Spirit was something that people could experience *today*.

Feeling uncomfortable, I quickly began to assess the situation and devise a plan to leave graciously. What I was unaware of, however, was that my husband had become captivated by the whole thing. Before I knew it, the people had formed a circle around him and were praying for him, speaking in a language that I had never heard before. Fear began to rise inside of me. I felt that somehow I needed to take control of the situation and get us out of there. After gathering my children, I went to get Rick. But I was too late.

Suddenly, they all stopped. That's when I noticed that Rick was now speaking in the same strange language! In an instant, my mind and emotions shifted into code red. I then clearly heard a voice inside my head say, *This is of the devil. Get Rick and get out of here right away!*

At this point, I was really struggling with what to do. Part of me wanted to stay, and part of me wanted to leave; but I felt like I couldn't leave. Just then, they all backed away from Rick, and I saw him. It looked as if someone had taken a five-gallon bucket of water and dumped it over his head, but there was no water on the floor. I looked around for a bucket, but I couldn't find one.

As I stood there both stunned and speechless, Rick looked up at me and said, "You have got to try this!" I thought to myself, *He has completely lost his mind. There's no way I am going to let those people pray for me. This has got to be some kind of a cult or something, and Rick has just gotten sucked into it. But how did they brainwash him so quickly?*

As best I could, I shook myself back to reality and tried to gather my wits. Still trying to find a way out of the situation, I noticed Rick was trying to tell me something. "Judy, something wonderful has just happened to me!" he said, but I wasn't really paying any attention to him.

Again, I heard a voice in my head scream, *Get out of here fast!* That's when I noticed something very different about Rick. I couldn't put my finger on it, but something was definitely different in his countenance. In the midst of all the chaos going on in my head, he seemed to be totally at peace. In bewilderment, I turned to him and said, "What's wrong with you?"

"Absolutely nothing," he replied. "I have never felt so good in my entire life. Honey, you have got to try this. It's real. I can't explain it, but it's real. Let these people pray for you."

I could not deny the fact that there was something definitely different about Rick. I knew him well enough to know that he would never fake anything. If he said that this was real and I should try it, then maybe there was something to it. Reluctantly, I agreed to let the people "lay hands on" me and pray that I would receive the baptism of the Holy Spirit. If Rick was wrong, I was sure going to give him trouble later!

As it turned out, he was right. Almost immediately, I was baptized in the Holy Spirit and began to speak in a new language. I was amazed! Something totally supernatural was happening to me, yet I was completely aware of everything that was going on.

When they stopped praying for me, I continued to pray in tongues just as Rick had done earlier. The same peace that I saw all over him was now all over me. The people who prayed for us then took time to explain some Scriptures on the baptism of the Holy Spirit, which really put me at ease. We went home that night not really sure of all that had happened. Little did we know that our lives were about to change dramatically.

The first major change I noticed was that I had an intense desire to know the Word of God—even more than I had before. Now when I sat down to read Scripture, I was able to understand passages I couldn't understand before. I also began to hear God's sweet, gentle voice speaking to me during my times of prayer. More and more I wanted to pray in tongues, and it seemed like the more I did, the stronger my faith grew.

Unfortunately, not everything changed overnight. Rick and I still had very heated arguments. Some were even more intense than before. But in time, this changed too, under the new dimension of God's power in which we had been submerged.

LIFE AFTER PENTECOST

It wasn't long before Rick and I realized there was much more to living a victorious Christian life than what we had been experiencing. We weren't quite sure how to handle this amazing thing that had just happened to us. We knew it was real, but we didn't know how to explain it to others.

The church we had been attending didn't believe in speaking in tongues, which definitely created a problem. There was just no way we could deny what had happened to us. Consequently, we began to search for a new church that would teach us how to live this new Spirit-filled life.

Meanwhile, our friend Norma strongly encouraged us to attend

a special conference in Gatlinburg, Tennessee. A man named
Norvel Hayes and a number of others, including Rodney Howard-
Browne, Dave Roberson and Elaine Hollmer, were all going to be
speaking during a special week of meetings. We took her advice
and went to the event.

Wow! What an unbelievable experience that was! We had never
seen or heard anything like it before. I was familiar with the gifts
of the Spirit, but I had never seen them manifested before. At first,
I was very skeptical and wondered if what I was seeing was real.
Although it seemed like a lot of emotionalism, I was still captivated
by it. Rick had always thought those kinds of people were crazy—
at least the ones he had seen on television. But now that he was baptized in the Holy Spirit and experiencing it firsthand, he knew that
it had to be God.

Truly, I was amazed to see God moving so powerfully right
before my eyes! I was deeply touched by the godly compassion with
which I saw His servants work. The things He revealed to the speakers, as well as the deliverances and healings He provided, were so
incredible I knew we had tapped into the genuine power of God.

PERSONALLY TOUCHED BY GOD'S HEALING POWER

While driving from Pennsylvania to Gatlinburg, I had a strange
pain in my chest the entire time. Initially, I just passed it off as
heartburn and didn't think too much of it. But the closer we got to
Gatlinburg, the worse the pain became. In fact, I had it the first two
days of the meetings and just couldn't get rid of it.

During one of the morning sessions, Elaine Hollmer was ministering, and God was using her to operate in what I now know to be
the word of knowledge. One by one, she pulled different people
from their seats and told them things about their lives. At first I
wondered if she was psychic. But then I realized that was not the
case; something was different.

She didn't just tell someone something about their life and then
walk away. She also laid her hands on them and prayed for them to
be healed. Amazingly, each person she prayed for was instantly

healed or delivered from whatever they were dealing with.

Eventually, she made her way to where Rick and I were sitting. Suddenly, her eyes caught a glimpse of me and she asked me to stand. I was terrified and that pain in my chest was now excruciating. She looked at me and said, "You are grieving from the loss of a loved one."

At that point, I thought for sure she was a phony because no one in my family had died for years. But then she put her hand right on the spot on my chest that was hurting and said, "You spirit of grief, come out!" At that moment, it was as if someone kicked my legs out from under me. I fell to the floor and lay there weeping for a few minutes. When I got up, I noticed right away that my chest no longer hurt. I had been healed.

When Elaine was finished with me, she turned to Rick and began telling him what God had shown her. Now, Rick had suffered off and on with bronchitis quite frequently. Just when it seemed like he was getting over it, it would come back. Not knowing any details about Rick's health, Elaine told him that there was something wrong with his blood and that was the reason he was sick so often. She then laid her hands on him, prayed and told him God was giving him all new blood. Amazed, I watched as my 6'4" husband fell to the floor in what appeared to be slow motion. Just like a giant oak tree that has fallen to the ground, he lay there motionless for quite some time. Slowly but surely, he got up and made his way back to where I was. To my knowledge, he has never had bronchitis since then.

RECEIVING REVELATION AND A NEW CHURCH HOME

Not only did we see the gifts of God's Spirit manifested in those meetings, but we also learned about the importance of worshipping God. Until then, I didn't know we were to worship God in private too. I thought that worshipping Him was only done at church. But that is not true, as Norvel Hayes explained so clearly from Scripture. Honestly, I couldn't understand why I had not seen it before. This truth was one of the most liberating things I had ever heard. With great appreciation, I raised my hands to heaven and worshipped God for the first time in my life on my knees in the middle of a hotel ballroom.

What a week that was! Rick and I learned so much and were hungry to learn more! God helped us find a new church close to our house that taught about how to live the Spirit-filled life. The people there worshipped the Lord passionately, prayed in tongues fervently and allowed the gifts of the Spirit to operate freely. Now going to church was fun—we actually looked forward to it!

Don't get me wrong. I wouldn't trade the days we spent in that Presbyterian church for anything. I learned so much about God from those wonderful people. But Rick and I both knew that God was doing something brand-new in our lives, and we were excited to embrace it.

About a month or so later while I was spending time in prayer, I suddenly realized what Elaine Hollmer meant when she said I was grieving over a lost loved one. It was the baby I had aborted in 1991. This revelation brought me to tears. As I wept, God did something amazing inside of me that I cannot put into words. For the first time since the abortion, I no longer had feelings of guilt and condemnation hanging over my head like a dark cloud. I was free!

Immediately, I sat down and wrote Elaine a letter, telling her what had happened. A year or so later, I actually had a chance to meet with her personally. After briefly retelling my story, I thanked her for helping me find freedom. We sat and cried together for awhile and talked about the goodness of God.

NEW HORIZONS OF UNDERSTANDING

As time passed, it became more and more evident how much Rick and I needed to learn about living the Spirit-filled life. We had no knowledge of demons, angels or the personal ministry of the Holy Spirit in our lives. With great enthusiasm and spiritual hunger, we dove into reading the Word and listening to teaching tapes.

We learned that each of us are three-part beings—spirit, soul and body. We also discovered that with God's help we can control the thoughts that come into our minds, choosing which ones we want to accept or reject. It was at this point that I also received a major revelation about the reality of Satan and how he and his team of demons had been bombarding my mind with thoughts of guilt and condemnation over the abortion. When I realized that it had been Satan that had tormented me so long, I became very upset with myself for putting up with his attack as long as I did.

Rick and I were also awakened to an understanding of the life-changing power and importance of our words. We had not known that the words of our lips could produce death or life (see Proverbs 18:21). What an eye-opening truth. It became quite apparent that we had a lot of things to repent of. But thank God for His great mercy and willingness to forgive. As His Word says, *If we confess our sins, He is faithful and just to forgive us of our sins and to cleanse us from all unrighteousness* (see 1 John 1:9 NKJV). What a wonderful gift!

By the power of God's Spirit living in us, we continued seeking the Lord and striving to live right. We learned about tithing, giving and the principle of sowing and reaping (see Galatians 6:6-10). We started tithing on our net income and eventually began tithing on our gross income and giving offerings on a regular basis. Over time, the Lord faithfully honored His Word and began to prosper us in every area of our lives.

We also learned the importance of walking in love and not harboring unforgiveness, bitterness and resentment toward others. When I began to think about all the people in my life who had hurt me, used me and betrayed me, I wasn't sure I could forgive them. Once again, God showed me how, and by His grace I did it. Although my feelings, or emotions, didn't line up with my will to forgive right away, God showed me that if I made a decision to forgive, eventually my feelings would line up with my will.

THE FIGHT IS STILL ON

Everything wasn't rosy yet, though. Rick and I were still having pretty bad fights, only now I was throwing tons of Scripture at him.

He hated when I did that, and I don't blame him. I was taking the Bible out of context, twisting the verses of scripture and using them against him. But I didn't know what I was doing. In my mind, most of our problems were his fault because he didn't spend enough time in prayer and studying the Word. What I desperately needed was a revelation of submission to authority and the fear of the Lord.

One particular night things really got heated between Rick and me. When he reached a point where he couldn't take anymore, he threw a barbell through the wall in our garage and then stormed out of the house with a loaded gun from the dresser. Satan was working overtime through our weaknesses—my uncontrollable mouth and fear of submitting to male authority and his feelings of rejection and insecurity.

Honestly, I thought he was just bluffing and blew him off. I assumed he'd be back, just like all the other times he had stormed out of the house in the past. The truth is, however, he was under the influence of a spirit of suicide, and he was determined to kill himself.

By God's grace, Rick reached out for help and called our friend Norma. After listening to him share what was going on, she was able to discern the spirit of suicide at work. She then prayed for Rick, binding the evil spirit and casting it out of Rick's life.

Meanwhile, I was at home, experiencing some pretty intense deliverance myself. In His mercy, the Lord showed me that I had opened the door to the demonic spirits of strife and destruction through the words I had been speaking. In desperation, I humbly cried out to Him for help. He graciously revealed to me the demonic spirits that were still lingering in my life and influencing my actions.

My former lifestyle of prostitution had opened my soul up to many demonic spirits. One by one as God revealed them to me, I repented for knowingly or unknowingly inviting them in and took authority over them, binding them and casting them out of my life. Their power over me began to break and the oppression lifted. The more I operated in the knowledge of the things of God, the more victory I had. When I focused my attention on Jesus and worshipped Him, I didn't have impure thoughts; they just disappeared.

P. 25

And the more I studied and listened to Christian teaching tapes, the more I realized that the problems Rick and I were experiencing were primarily coming from me, not him. Thankfully, I eventually got a revelation of the principle of submission to authority and how God desires wives to respond to and treat their husbands. God is still working on me in this area of my life and probably will be for quite some time.

God is such a good Father! Just as good parents give mercy and grace to their children as they grow, God does the same for us. He won't give us more than we can handle and He doesn't expect more of us than what we are able to give. I don't know what would have happened to Rick and me had God not baptized us in His Holy Spirit. All I know is, I'm really glad He did. It changed our lives forever!

Chapter 7

A WOLF IN SHEEP'S CLOTHING
The Enemy's Attempt to Deceive
and Derail God's Plan

FIRST IMPRESSIONS CAN BE DECEIVING

In July of 1996, Rick and I decided to go to Pastor Rod Parsley's camp meeting in Columbus, OH. This particular conference was scheduled during the week of July 4, and it included several speakers and services. The church was very large and could seat about 5,000 people.

At this point, we had been baptized in the Holy Spirit for a little over a year and were still passionately pursuing God with all of our hearts. We didn't want to miss a thing. To ensure we got good seats as close to the front as possible, we tried to get there early for each service. What made the camp meeting even more enjoyable was that they had wonderful classes for children. This enabled us to concentrate more fully on the ministry we were receiving.

The first night we were there, we met and sat next to a lady named Mona.* She was in her mid to late 50s and lived in Florida. She seemed like a really sweet lady and we enjoyed talking with her that evening.

We had made it a habit to arrive early at each service and sit in the same area, and so did Mona. Consequently, we had plenty of time to talk with her and get to know her. After the last service at the end of the week, we hugged her and said good-bye, remarking about how much we had been blessed by the entire camp meeting. Rick and I then packed up the car and headed back to Pennsylvania.

A GLIMPSE INTO THE SPIRIT REALM

I was very excited about getting home that evening because we were having all-night prayer at church. Once we arrived at home, we got everything settled and went to church.

I distinctly remember being at the altar worshipping God when I heard a voice inside of me say, *Turn around*. The voice was so clear that I thought someone was standing behind me speaking. So I turned around and saw someone or something standing in the back of the church. It looked like a person, but there was something else there too.

As I started to walk toward the person, I noticed that it was Mona, the lady that we had met at the camp meeting in Ohio. But I also noticed something else as I was walking toward her. I saw what looked like a large lizard standing behind her. The best way I can describe it is that it was rather transparent, almost like it was standing inside of her.

When she opened her mouth and spoke to me, a lizard-like tongue about six feet long came rolling out of her mouth. It was forked on the end and it was lashing back and forth. Needless to say, this totally freaked me out. I had no idea what was going on. I was scared, but fascinated at the same time. Again, I heard a voice inside of me say, *She is under the influence of a lying spirit. Do not listen to anything she says*. Almost instantly, the lizard-like creature disappeared. Was I perhaps being warned about Mona through this *spiritual vision* even though I was not sure what it meant at the time?

When I finally reached the back of the church, I greeted her and asked her what she was doing here. She said that God had told her to come to Pennsylvania Dutch Country. I couldn't believe it. What was God doing?

This lady was very confident and charismatic in nature, yet she came across innocent in her demeanor—like a mom or an aunt that you feel comfortable with. She had led a very fascinating life, and it was intriguing to talk to her. Well, as you may have guessed, the other people at the prayer service really liked her. They were convinced that God had sent her just like she claimed, and we ended up having a wonderful prayer service.

CLASH OF THE SPIRITUAL TITANS

Mona followed me home, and Rick was surprised to see her when we arrived. She ended up staying with us for about a week. I enjoyed listening to her talk about the Bible and intercessory prayer. She seemed to be so knowledgeable about the things of God. She reminded me of another good friend from Connecticut named Mary Jenkins.

I had met Mary at a Norvel Hayes conference a few years earlier. She was about eighty-five years old and had grown up under Smith Wigglesworth's ministry. Mother Jenkins, as I called her, was full of the love of God and like a spiritual mother to me. She operated in tremendous godly wisdom and discernment. I loved her very much.

I thought it would be wonderful for Mother Jenkins and our newfound friend Mona to meet and get to know each other. So Mona agreed to come back to Pennsylvania and visit us when Mother Jenkins was in town. And this time when she came, she said she would bring her daughter. I was so excited.

When Mother Jenkins arrived, I began to tell her about Mona. Almost immediately, I could tell that she sensed something wasn't right. The more I told her about her, the quieter she became. When I asked her what was wrong, she said, "Nothin' honey." But I knew Mother Jenkins well enough to know that something was bothering her because she had never acted that way before.

As soon as Mona arrived, I introduced her to Mother Jenkins. Almost immediately, Mona began acting very strange. I wondered what the problem was. Was she jealous of my friendship with Mother Jenkins? Did she just not like her? Or was it something else?

A couple of days went by, and then Mother Jenkins pulled me aside and told me there was something wrong with Mona, but she couldn't quite put her finger on it yet. Until this time, I had not told her about what I had seen in the back of our church the night Mona arrived, so I shared it with her. This brought more clarity to the situation for her about what was actually going on.

Oddly enough, Mona eventually pulled me aside and basically told me the same thing about Mother Jenkins. She said, "I don't want to tell you what to do, but that other lady is not your friend. I don't know what she is up to, but it is definitely not good."

Shortly thereafter, I began to notice that Mona became defensive whenever Mother Jenkins challenged her on her interpretation of certain Scriptures. More and more, it became obvious that the two did not like one another. At that point I didn't know what to do. I was very confused. I loved Mother Jenkins and deeply respected her godly wisdom and insight. On the other hand, I really liked Mona and thought she was spiritually mature. However, I couldn't ignore the uneasiness and turmoil in my spirit about her. I didn't know what was causing it or how to get rid of it. I definitely needed to hear from God.

When it came time for Mother Jenkins to go home, I brought her to the train station and saw her off. I will never forget the deep concern I saw in her eyes and the stern nature of her voice that day. She warned me to pray about everything and not to make any move without being in full agreement with Rick.

FALLING DEEPER INTO DECEPTION

When I returned to my house, Mona was still there. By this time, it seemed as though she had taken over. With an air of spiritual superiority, she told me about demon spirits that she claimed to see attached to a bowl on my kitchen counter. Naïve and spiritually immature, I became envious of her "discernment."

She came with us to church several times, and just about everyone loved her. She spoke so authoritatively about the Scriptures and even played the piano on the platform a few times. I was convinced that God had sent her into my life to mentor me.

When it came time for her to go, she asked if I would like to take my children and come spend some time in Florida with her and her daughter. She said she had plenty of room and it would give me a chance to get away. Rick and I thought it was a good idea, so we packed some things in her Mercedes and off we went.

Her house in Florida was beautiful. We quickly settled in and enjoyed the first few days together. It wasn't until about the third day that I began to notice I was spending a lot of time going to the bathroom. Although I wasn't eating anything different than normal, it seemed like nothing I ate agreed with me. This had never happened to me before and I didn't understand it. I tried to ignore it, but it was obvious something was wrong with me.

In the meantime, I began to notice that Mona favored my son over my daughter. She even bought him things and didn't buy anything for her. At first, I thought it was because she had her daughter with her all the time and she missed having her son around. (Her son visited once while we were there, but I don't think their relationship was very good.) I explained to her that Victoria was very sensitive, and while I was happy for her to buy things for Christian, she really needed to treat them equally.

To my amazement, Mona replied saying that my daughter was spoiled and shouldn't expect so much. Her shocking remarks didn't end there. At one point, she told me that Rick wasn't doing a very good job of leading our family and that I should leave him and come stay with her. He probably wouldn't even miss me.

It was then that I started putting everything together and knew I needed to get out of there. Immediately, I called Rick and told him to come and get me. I explained to him what was going on, including the things she was saying about him and the kids. Unfortunately, he couldn't come for a few days. He was working on closing one particular real estate deal that he had been working on for quite some time.

As I waited, I became tormented by fear. One night, after we had turned off all the lights to go to bed, I saw Mona seated in her living room. The moonlight was shining through the big living room window and reflecting on her face. In a very eerie way, she looked at me and smiled. What I saw then was the same thing I saw the night she showed up in our church.

Finally, Rick arrived and I was never so relieved to see him. I packed our things in our car as fast as I could and we left. I didn't let Mona know that there was anything wrong because I wasn't sure what she would do. She was so convincing and likeable, I almost felt bad for thinking the thoughts I had about her. But I could not ignore the strange things that I saw and felt when she was around.

TRYING TO SPIN A NEW WEB

When we returned home, things became normal once again. However, Mona was not out of the picture. She called quite frequently, continuing to express interest and concern for me and my family. In a backward way, she even apologized for saying the things she had said about Rick and my kids. I forgave her and extended her the benefit of the doubt because that's what I thought I was supposed to do.

During this whole ordeal with Mona, our church was in the process of selecting a new senior pastor. Our former pastor had abruptly announced one Sunday that it was his final service and that he was resigning, effective immediately. They had actually started the interviewing process while Mona was visiting, and she had met the man we voted in as the new pastor.

Time passed and Mona planned to come for another visit. I felt I was stronger now and that I would be able to keep things under control. I wasn't going to let her get away with the things she had done when we were together previously.

When she arrived, things seemed to go fine at first. I was singing and playing the keyboard in church as I had been for quite some time, and occasionally Mona would sing and play too. She was very good and most of the people seemed to enjoy her playing. However, some of the other members of the worship team didn't like when she played and didn't approve of her being on the platform.

When the new pastor arrived, he asked if Mona and I would lead praise and worship the first Sunday he ministered. I was thrilled! I had never been asked to do that before. Excitedly, we showed up early on Sunday morning and began preparing. However, some of the other worship team members were unaware of the new pastor's request, and they were already rehearsing in the sanctuary. After I explained to them that the pastor had asked Mona and me to lead worship, they reluctantly agreed to let us prepare.

Mona then told me that God was moving her to Pennsylvania to be a part of a church and she hoped it would be mine. Unfortunately, after the service, the pastor told her that he didn't have peace about her leading worship. He expressed appreciation for her willingness to serve, but he didn't believe that it was God's perfect will for her to be there. As you might imagine, she was disappointed and I was embarrassed.

Again, she told me that she was positive that God had told her to come to Pennsylvania and become a part of a church. Deeply disturbed, she began to say that our new pastor was not hearing from God. She then cautioned us about being a part of a church that had such a controlling pastor. Rick and I listened and believed she had some valid points. Before long, we began to think and pray about whether or not God wanted us to remain at the church.

That's when Mona had a "revelation." She announced that she realized why God had sent her to Pennsylvania: to start a church! And Rick and I were supposed to be involved in it. As a matter of fact, we were supposed to pastor it.

As far-fetched as this may seem, please understand that Rick and I fervently wanted God's will. And we honestly believed that Mona had been sent to us from the Lord. Unfortunately, we were not spiritually mature enough to recognize what was going on.

ONLY TRUTH CAN DESTROY DECEPTION

With our eyes clouded by a web of deception, Rick and I decided that Mona was right and immediately began looking for a place to begin a new church. It was at that point that people we knew began to come to us and say things like, "What are you doing? Don't you see what this woman is up to?" I can honestly say we didn't see it. We were greatly deceived and totally unaware of it. Everything Mona said seemed to make sense to us.

As you read this, you may be thinking, *How foolish and blind could you have been?* The answer is, yes, we were blinded. I cannot tell you how the enemy did it, but he had us convinced that we were doing the right thing. That's how deception works. We could have saved ourselves so much turmoil and embarrassment if we would have just taken the time to seek the Lord and listen to His counsel!

By God's grace and His mercy, our eyes were opened and we

finally realized that we were headed down the wrong road. We totally severed our relationship with Mona, and immediately were able to see how she was manipulating us and controlling us. It was as if blinders had been removed and we could see clearly.

Rick and I both recognize now how the enemy used Mona to try and get us off the path of our divine destiny. We learned many important lessons, including the importance of staying in close, regular fellowship with the Lord. We learned we must also guard ourselves from being more drawn to a person than to God Himself. Furthermore, I learned the importance of taking heed to warnings like the ones I got from trusted friends and from the unusual *spiritual vision* I had experienced. Rick and I are forever grateful to God for our true friends who faithfully told us the truth that set us free from the deception of the enemy.

*Mona is not this woman's real name; it has been changed to protect her true identity.

Chapter 8

EXPERIENCING A SEASON OF EXPONENTIAL GROWTH
Ministry and Mentoring
at Joyce Meyer Ministries

DISCOVERING JOYCE MEYER

With Mona finally out of our lives, Rick and I recommitted ourselves to our church and made amends with anyone who was hurt during the time she was there. We continued to grow and serve in ministry and truly enjoy the wonderful gift God gave us in our church. For the first time, life was really going well—our marriage was healthy, the children were doing great, and the real estate business was thriving.

At that point, I decided to get a certified nurse's aide license to enable me to care for the elderly. Within a short amount of time, I was working for three different nursing agencies at once—sometimes working sixteen-hour shifts. I cannot explain why I wanted to do this, other than it was an opportunity for me to minister and it was a much needed service in our community. It also provided us with regular paychecks, which is something that is not always guaranteed in the real estate industry.

During this season of my life, I began watching as much Christian television as I could. That's when I came across a woman minister named Joyce Meyer. At first, I thought she was pretty rough, but she always seemed to be speaking right to me. Whatever I was going through at the time, she would be ministering on that very thing. It never ceased to amaze me. She had been through so many troubles, including some of the same things I had been through. But God had brought her out of each of them. Her life became a real inspiration, and I wanted what she had.

I wasn't the only one being helped by Joyce's ministry. God was using her to help Rick, too. Two of her books, *The Root of Rejection* and *Battlefield of the Mind*, truly transformed his life. Through *Battlefield of the Mind*, Rick learned about the ongoing fight in our thoughts between the Holy Spirit living in us and the enemy, Satan. He realized that it was Satan giving him the crazy, impure thoughts he was thinking, and then condemning him for having them. By God's grace, Rick learned to be prepared to do battle with the enemy by knowing the truth of God's Word and speaking it to counter and cast down the lies of Satan. Finally, he began to experience freedom from condemnation like never before.

Needless to say, we began ordering Joyce's tapes and books on a regular basis, and in 1996 we became partners with her ministry. I faithfully watched her as often as I could because what she said ministered to me deeply. I also read her ministry magazine, which we received monthly. Indeed, Rick and I had entered a new season of spiritual growth and it was evident.

A PROMISING SEED OF CHANGE

One month while looking through Joyce's magazine, I distinctly remember seeing an ad for employment opportunities on the back cover. I thought, *How awesome would it be to work at Joyce Meyer Ministries! That would be too good to be true!* Almost immediately, I dismissed the idea as just wishful thinking. I knew that Rick had been born and raised in Lancaster, Pennsylvania, and had no intention of leaving. He was prospering in real estate and I was working steadily as a nurse's aide. It would make no sense at all to leave what we had to go work at a ministry.

My feelings were confirmed by Rick's initial reaction to the idea. "So what?" he said. "What does that ad in the magazine have to do with us?" Reluctantly I agreed. However, not knowing exactly what God might be doing, I threw up a simple prayer: "God, if it is

Your will for Rick and me to work at Joyce Meyer Ministries, then I pray that You would put that ad back in the magazine. If I see that ad again, I will call and ask for the applications."

Well, the ad was not in the next month's magazine. I was kind of disappointed, but like I told myself before, *it would be too good to be true*. So I pushed it out of my mind for about six months. Then the ad showed up again. Suddenly, I was reminded of my prayer, so I brought it back to Rick's attention and called for applications to be sent to us.

Little did I know, but God had planted a seed in Rick's heart when I first mentioned the idea to him. Through a series of circumstances, including major changes and disappointments in his real estate business, God worked on him to be open to the idea and willing to act on it. In a matter of months, he had become so frustrated and discouraged with his business that by the time I brought him the applications, he knew in his heart it was right to send them.

Still battling with some thoughts and feelings of resistance, Rick prayed, "Well God, if You really want this to happen, You are going to have to make it happen." We filled out the applications, mailed them, and waited to see what would happen.

NEW LIFE BEGINS TO BUD

Sure enough, we received a phone call from the ministry shortly thereafter. I was so excited! After an in-depth interview by phone, they asked if we would come to their headquarters in St. Louis, Missouri, for a personal interview. Wow! Everything seemed to be happening so fast. But since we felt in our hearts like God was directing things, we went along with it and made arrangements to go to St. Louis. Once we secured a sitter for the kids, we headed to Missouri.

When we arrived at the ministry, we were both very nervous. But the sincere love and kindness of Christ in the employees we met quickly put us at ease. During the interview, we talked about many things, including relocating to Missouri. One thing that I purposely did not talk about, however, was my former lifestyle. I was afraid if they knew that I used to be a prostitute, they would never hire me. Although I kept quiet about it during the interview process, eventually I would reveal this part of my past.

All in all, the interviews went well. Once they were done, we returned to Lancaster and waited to hear from them. A couple of weeks passed and we received the phone call we had been waiting for. I remember it like it was yesterday. Rick came to a house where I was caring for an elderly man and shared the good news with me. They asked if we would like to relocate to St. Louis and work full-time at the ministry. I couldn't believe it. They really wanted us, and we were elated!

Once our emotions settled down, we realized the enormous task that lay ahead of us. We owned four houses that would need to be sold in a sluggish real estate market, and we had $30,000 of credit card debt. On top of that, we knew we would be taking a cut in pay to work for the ministry, but we didn't care. We knew in our hearts that we were doing the right thing, so God would take care of us.

GOD'S FINGERPRINTS ARE ALL OVER IT

At the time Rick and I were hired, Dave and Joyce had recently sent their partners information about the new ministry headquarters they were building, asking people to pray about investing in the project. Right away, Rick and I knew in our hearts that this was an opportunity from God to become debt free. We prayed and agreed about the size of the "financial seed" we would sow into the ministry headquarters. We sent it, and in less than six months, we sold all four properties and paid off all the credit card debt! Amazingly, we were moving to St. Louis debt free!

Unfortunately, not everyone was as excited about this opportunity as we were. A number of people thought that we were crazy and made fun of us. Rick got a farewell card from his real estate office that was signed by everyone, and someone had written, "You'll be back in eighteen months." Another person that wasn't thrilled about our move was Rick's mom. But because we both knew in our hearts that God was directing our steps, we were determined to obey Him and not be swayed by anything or anybody.

I still remember the last Sunday we were in our little church. The pastor called Rick and me to the front and announced to everyone that we were leaving. He had counseled us not to go, stating that most people who have visions of working for large ministries never get to travel with them. Instead, they often end up working in the phone department or the warehouse. Nevertheless, he knew we had made up our minds to go and he wanted the congregation to pray for us before we left.

During his prayer, a message in tongues was given, and our pastor got the interpretation. Through his own mouth, God confirmed that *He Himself* had opened this door of opportunity with Joyce Meyer Ministries, and we shouldn't let any man talk us out of it.

Over and over, God confirmed that this move was of Him and that we were in His perfect will. Every business deal that Rick needed to happen, happened. All of our investment properties sold, which enabled him to fulfill every business related promise he had made. I had even prayed for a specific apartment in St. Louis and God gave it to us. But the fingerprints of God's presence in our move didn't stop there.

The day we moved in it was pouring down rain. The visibility was so bad we could barely see the exit sign while we were driving. Thankfully, we managed to get off the freeway and arrive at the apartment complex. My parents, as well as my aunt and uncle, were there to help us. With the rain still pouring down, I got mad and prayed, "God, You asked us to move out here and now all my stuff is going to get soaked. We are trying to obey You. Can You please do something about this rain!"

The moment we opened the back of the moving van, the rain completely stopped and didn't start again until the last box was being unloaded. Without question, God was in this move.

A WHOLE NEW WORLD

Finally, we had arrived and were getting settled in Missouri. It was the summer of 1998, and it was now time to start working in our new positions at the ministry. Can you guess where Rick and I started?

Yep! I was placed in the phone department, and he was placed in the warehouse! Believe it or not, I thought it was quite funny. It really didn't bother us. We were just thrilled to be there.

The truth is, our lives were great. Even the cut in pay didn't matter. All of our needs were met, and we never went without anything. Rick's work that first year was so rewarding and relaxing. The hardest thing he had to remember to do was punch a time clock every day—something he hadn't done for fifteen years or more. When he left work, he didn't have to take work home with him. For the first time since we could remember, we had time to do things together as a family that we couldn't do before.

It wasn't long after Rick and I arrived that we were both promoted. He became assistant supervisor in the warehouse, and I was asked to work in the executive office as a secretary to Dave Meyer's assistant. Of course, we were thrilled!

The Lord also led us to a wonderful new church—Life Christian Church. Interestingly, this church was where Joyce was an associate pastor before entering full-time ministry on her own. Once we were plugged in, we quickly became active. I became a part of the choir and Rick ran the television cameras.

Life was great! I was learning so much by working in the executive office. Like few people, I got a personal and up-close view of how Dave and Joyce lived behind the scenes. I learned firsthand how a godly woman should treat her husband by observing both Joyce and Roxane Schermann, another wonderful woman of God who was the general manager at the time.

I did experience challenging times of spiritual growth, though, and they were hard. When I saw how differently Joyce and Roxane thought and acted, I said to myself, *I will never get this! I have so much to learn about how to live a godly life.*

I'll never forget the time I was corrected about having a prideful attitude. I thought I would die. It hurt so much I could hardly speak. I knew they were right, but I was humiliated and embarrassed by what I had done. Thankfully, my desire to grow spiritually superseded my feelings, and I received their correction. I read the books they gave me and prayed earnestly for God to deliver me from pride and help me develop a submissive attitude.

Joyce's teaching series on submission to authority helped me tremendously. For the first time, I realized that submitting to authority is actually very liberating. I also learned that if I submitted to the authority that God placed over me, He would make sure that I was protected. This was a major change in my thinking that only God could bring.

CLIMBING HIGHER IN THE KINGDOM

Rick was also growing by leaps and bounds, and before long he was promoted again—this time to the position of manager of what is now called the distribution department. I had served in the executive office for eighteen months, when one day Dave and Joyce pulled me aside and asked me if I would like to manage the conference department. My initial reaction was, "I don't know anything about how to manage a department." Besides that, I loved working closely with Dave and Joyce, and I loved being around Roxane. I didn't want to leave that atmosphere. But God had something different in mind.

After Rick and I prayed about it, we knew it was God's will for me to take the position. When I met with Dave and Joyce again, I accepted the job. I must say, my emotions were definitely not in the decision. I tried to convince myself that that was where I needed to be, but it wasn't working very well. I remember lying on my living room floor one night, crying out to God and saying, "If You don't help me do this, all I am going to make is a big mess! Please give me wisdom, give me ideas, give me creativity and give me favor! Help me to not be a respecter of persons. I am totally relying and depending on Your help!" And help me He did—although not the way I thought He would.

Within two or three months of taking the position as the conference department manager, everyone in my department quit! One by one, they left. Needless to say, I was back on the floor of my living room, crying out to God for explanation. The devil tried to convince me it was my fault—that I was a terrible manager, and that's why everyone was leaving. But that wasn't the case. God was assembling a new team for a new season.

Just as they left one by one, God brought in new people one by one. These were special individuals handpicked by Him to form a new team for the new thing He had in store. Looking back, I still stand amazed at what God accomplished in that conference department through the anointing of His Holy Spirit and our desperation for His Presence. He is truly amazing!

TRUE FULFILLMENT FROM AN UNEXPECTED PLACE

About three years after we had been attending Life Christian Church, God uprooted us and transplanted us at the St. Louis Dream Center, the inner-city outreach of Joyce Meyer Ministries. Ironically, just as I didn't want to leave the executive office to manage the conference department, I didn't want to leave Life Christian Church. Nevertheless, we knew in our hearts it was God, and if it was God, He would bless it.

When we met with the senior pastors of the Dream Center, we shared our testimony with them. Upon hearing it, they smiled real big and said they had been praying for someone like us to head up their midnight outreach to prostitutes, pimps and drug dealers. At that moment, we knew we had made the right decision.

We began going out every Friday night from 11 p.m. to 3 a.m. to some of the worst parts of St. Louis, looking for prostitutes we could minister to. I can't put into words how happy I was. I had never felt so fulfilled in all my life. God had done such a mighty work in me that I could look at the girls we met and say, "You don't have to live like this. If God brought me out of prostitution, He can bring you out too." I loved them, cried with them and told them that Jesus died for them and had a great plan for their life.

Some listened and some didn't. Some were so afraid of what their pimps might do, they didn't dare talk to us, but that didn't matter. Rick and I talked to the pimps, too! Some of them even got saved! We talked to transvestites, homeless people and anyone who would listen. In a period of about eighteen months, we formed great relationships with many of these people.

Sometimes other Christians asked us, "Aren't you scared to go to those kinds of places?" By God's grace, I could look them straight in the eye and honestly say we were never afraid. Oh, there were several times when I knew we were in danger, but we were never afraid. God gave us a special deposit of His holy boldness every time we went out to minister, and we knew He would protect us. We used wisdom in every situation we encountered, but ultimately we knew that God had our backs!

THE ULTIMATE TEST OF FAITH

One day, unexpectedly, God asked me to lay down the ministry to the prostitutes. At that time, I really didn't understand it. It made absolutely no sense to me whatsoever. I just couldn't comprehend this decision on His part. *Have I missed something?* I prayerfully cried. *What is going on? What are You doing, God?* As hard as it was, I knew in my heart it was the right thing to do. I wasn't aware of it then, but God was about to do more "spiritual surgery" on me that I desperately needed.

At that point, He instructed me to study nothing but the love of God for the next twelve months. I had no problem loving non-Christians. When they messed up or did something wrong, I knew it was because they didn't know any better. However, when I saw Christians doing something wrong—things that God would never let *me* get away with—I was enraged. Without question, I had a problem loving God's people.

So, I began to intensely study the love of God, devouring both tapes and books on the subject. I prayed about love, confessed Scriptures about love, and cried out to God to help me love His people.

During that time, going to church at the Dream Center had really lost its luster. All the joy and peace about being there and serving there were lost. On top of that, it became increasingly difficult for Rick and me to receive ministry from the pastor. As painful as it was, we made the decision to leave the Dream Center completely.

God in His mercy led us to another church closer to our home where we plugged in for two to three years. In that season, God continued to minister to us and through us. Eventually, we would return to the Dream Center to serve in ministry again.

Chapter 9

UNEXPECTED GAINS & LOSSES
How Matters of Life and Death Directed Our Path

A HISTORY OF ILLNESS

My story would not be complete without a snapshot of some of the health issues my family and I have had to deal with over the years. And if there was anyone who understood the debilitating effects of disease, it was definitely my mom. Heart trouble was prevalent on her side of the family, and she had problems with her heart for as long as I can remember—especially when I was in high school. Although, the doctors had her on a lot of medication, she never lost her enthusiasm for life. She and my dad loved playing country music with their friends and visiting nursing home residents to entertain them.

Eventually, the condition of her heart became so bad that she needed a transplant. I was living in San Diego with my brother at the time and felt pretty helpless. Jerry and I talked with my parents on the phone every once in a while, but we never went to see them. Our relationship with them was okay, but we were not very close.

In 1989, a donor was found and a date for the transplant was set. The procedure was successfully performed without complications at a hospital in Iowa. Sadly, though, the doctors only gave her three to five years to live. To help prevent her body from rejecting the new heart, she had to take fistfuls of medication every day. Although she was not encouraged with the doctor's diagnosis, it didn't seem to bother her a bit. She and my dad continued to travel to California every winter and play their country music just as they had done before. They even enjoyed doing dances in the little retirement community they lived in.

My brother and I began to visit them every now and then while I was still living in San Diego. I was so proud of them for being so courageous and determined. At the same time, I was extremely ashamed of my drug and alcohol lifestyle. Never once did I share with them any information about this part of my life. I just didn't see any point in it. I learned later that they knew about it all along, but they never said anything to me. I guess they thought I was an adult, and I had the choice to do what I wanted.

OUR LAST MEMORABLE MOMENTS WITH MOM

About ten years after Mom's heart transplant, her heart had become considerably weak. Although she had beaten the odds, she reached a point where she could no longer travel and began spending weeks at a time in and out of the hospital. It was 1999, and Rick and I were married, living in St. Louis and working at Joyce Meyer Ministries. I faithfully tried to comfort her and keep the lines of communication open, frequently calling her and assuring her that everything was going the be alright. I knew in my heart, however, that we needed to make a trip to go see her, and soon.

One day during the summer, Rick and I decided to drive to Iowa to see her in the hospital. We wanted her to be able to visit with the kids and have some special time with her while she was still alive. When we arrived at the hospital, I was overwhelmed by how severe her condition was. It was very difficult for me to see her lying in the bed, but I tried to be strong.

As I watched my mom color pictures with her two grandchildren, I fought back the tears. She so enjoyed being with them. She even had one of the nurses bring her a guitar, and she played country music with her roommate! I cherish those memories. But what I cherish even more is the privilege Rick and I had in leading both my mom and dad in a prayer of salvation. I had determined in my heart not to leave until they had heard the message of the Gospel and prayed to invite Jesus into their hearts, and that is just what they did.

A few months passed, and mom was out of the hospital. I was so thrilled that she was still hanging on and we would get to see her again. We were planning to spend Thanksgiving with her and Dad in Iowa. But just days before we were to arrive, we received a phone call from him saying she had taken a turn for the worst. The day before we got there, she died. Initially, I was mad at God because I wanted to see her again, but He had other plans.

Gratefully, I was granted the opportunity to give Mom's eulogy at the funeral. I felt it was best to talk about all the positive and funny things she did. Almost everyone knew my parents. Mom was actually quite famous around the area—partly for her country music talent and partly because of the longevity of her heart transplant. I had the privilege of telling all our family and friends who gathered that day the greatest thing my mom ever did. It was not earning multiple awards for her yodeling or guitar playing; it was the day she prayed and asked Jesus Christ to forgive her of her sins and come live in her heart as her Lord and Savior. "I will miss my mom very much," I said. "But because of her salvation, I will see her again."

THE AFTERMATH OF THE FUNERAL

With my mom gone, my dad became an emotional mess. Not only was he dealing with Mom's death, he was also coping with numerous health problems, including diabetes, a colostomy and nerve disorders. Thankfully, he decided to come to St. Louis and spend some time with us. He stayed with Rick and me for about a month, and Aunt Vickie stayed with us too.

That's when things took a rather strange turn. My dad informed us that he and my mom had made arrangements for a mutual friend of theirs to start taking care of him after she passed away. This lady knew the severity of my dad's medical issues and was willing to provide the daily care he needed. Aunt Vickie, Rick and I thought this was a little odd, but it seemed to be what he wanted to do. So he left St. Louis and moved in with his female friend out west and lived there for a short time.

The next thing we knew, they got married and moved back to the family farm where I grew up in Iowa. They only lived there a short time—just long enough to get things in order and put the farm up for sale. I was very emotional the day everything was put up for auction and sold to the highest bidder. My stomach turned as I watched people rummage through all the things I had spent half my life looking at. Without question, that was a very difficult day, but by God's grace and Rick by my side, I managed to make it through. When it was all said and done, my dad and my newfound stepmother moved to the West Coast to be closer to her family. Honestly, it all happened so fast, it was hard to digest.

Through the whole process and afterward, God dealt with me regarding my relationship with my dad and stepmother. I learned some difficult lessons in humility and dependence on God to be my vindicator. At times, it was a daily effort to stay in control and do the right thing. I wanted desperately to be obedient to God in caring for my dad and showing him honor. With His strength, I determined in my heart to maintain the right attitude and press on—even when my dad continued to bring up my past failures.

CHALLENGES CLOSER TO HOME

Not only did I gain a stepmother after mom passed away, but I also gained a full-time live-in mother-in-law one year after we moved to St. Louis. Rick's mom was just not coping well living alone in Lancaster, Pennsylvania, so we invited her to move in with us. We had just purchased a house and the timing seemed perfect. Boy was my life about to change!

We gave her the master bedroom, and Rick and I slept in the basement. It was nothing but the grace of God that got me through the next several years. God used my mother-in-law to expose a number of things that needed to change in my character. In many areas, we were complete opposites: While we slept at night, she slept during the day. While we wanted to eat healthy, she primarily wanted junk food. Things became so difficult at one point, I began to pray, "Just take me home, Lord, and do it now! I will never make it!"

I had no problem dealing with her when she lived a few states away, but there was no escaping her now! Everywhere I went, she was there. Isn't it funny how God uses rough and tough situations and people in our lives to act as sandpaper to smooth us out? Funny may not be the correct word, because it certainly doesn't seem funny when we're going through it!

Nearly six years passed, and it was August of 2005. The time had come when Rick and I had to place my mother-in-law into a nursing home. At that point she required extensive care and attention almost around the clock—care that we were no longer able to provide for her. Throughout the entire time she stayed with us, I truly grew to love her. Many things in *her* character never changed, but they did in mine. And for that, I am eternally grateful to her.

IT LOOKS LIKE CANCER

Right in the middle of my mother-in-law's extended stay with us, I became concerned about a funny bump in my belly. It had been there for quite some time, but because it didn't hurt, I didn't think much about it. I hated going to the doctor, especially an OB/GYN. It had been about eight years since my last visit, and that was just fine with me. Rick, however, was concerned about the bump because it seemed to be growing. My staff at work was also troubled over it. So after their incessant questioning and nagging, I reluctantly made an appointment. But I insisted that Rick go with me.

Within what seemed to be less than ten seconds, the doctor immediately determined that there was definitely something wrong with me. To better understand what he was dealing with, he abruptly cleared the ultrasound room and had me go in. I didn't like the harsh tone of his voice or the rude way in which he was bossing everyone around. Nevertheless, I complied with his requests.

The ultrasound clearly showed a large mass in my abdomen. The doctor said that although he didn't know for sure, it looked very much like a cancerous ovarian tumor. He recommended immediate surgery to remove it.

At this point, I was dumbfounded by the unbelievable chain of events that was rapidly taking place. I looked at the doctor and politely informed him who I was. "I am the Conference Department manager for Joyce Meyer Ministries, and in just a few weeks, we will be holding our largest annual convention. Thousands of women from all over the world will be coming. My team and I will be coordinating the event. I simply don't have time to have surgery right now. It will have to wait." Needless to say, he was not impressed or moved by my words.

One of the things that I struggled with the most throughout the whole ordeal was the fact that he was talking to me about cancer. He wasn't talking to me about somebody else possibly having cancer; he was talking to *me*—Judy Lamborn—about possibly having cancer. I had prayed with people who had cancer and gone through cancer situations with many others, but this was different. I was not in control of this situation, and I didn't like it one bit.

Again, my faith and the faith of my family were severely tested. I remember turning to Rick at one point and saying, "Well, either we believe in what the Bible says, or we don't. I can't believe that God delivered me from everything He has delivered me from just to let me die in the clutches of cancer at the age of thirty-seven." Right then and there, we joined hands and prayed and placed the whole thing in God's hands.

Although I tenaciously tried to negotiate with and persuade the doctor to do the surgery after our women's convention, he wouldn't budge. The surgery was scheduled for two weeks later. During that time of waiting, I had to choose to reject thousands of negative thoughts that bombarded my mind. I was determined not to allow the situation to interrupt the call of God on my life. I felt fear but I was determined to overcome it. Because I had walked through numerous situations like this with others, I knew the kinds of thoughts and words that I needed to focus my mind on and fill my mouth with.

I still remember the day in September 2003 when I told the management team at the ministry about my planned surgery. Usually, Joyce attended the meeting, but at that time she was on vacation. I didn't think much of it; I just decided I would tell her about it when she returned. In the meantime, preparations needed to be made in my department, as well as other departments, because I would not be present at the convention.

A day or two later, my phone rang, and much to my surprise, it was Joyce Meyer on the other end. By now, I had been working with her for about four years, and I had really grown to love and respect her greatly. I knew firsthand how full her schedule was and how valuable her vacation time must be. The fact that she interrupted it to call me and make sure that I was okay really blessed my socks off! After I briefly shared the situation with her and told her I wasn't afraid, she prayed with me. Indeed, that is one treasured phone call and prayer I will never forget.

SURGERY AND RECOVERY

Rick and I told the kids what was going to happen the night before the surgery. After we did, my daughter looked at me in a way I had never seen before. She grabbed my hand and told me, "It's not cancer, Mommy. You're gonna be just fine." And with that, she walked out of the room. Without question, I will always know that God spoke to me through my daughter that night, and no one can convince me otherwise.

The morning of the surgery, I had total peace. A short time after they wheeled me in and began operating, the doctor called Rick, who was in the waiting room, from a phone inside the operating room. He told him they had removed the tumor and they didn't think it was cancerous. However, they were going to send it to pathology to have it tested to be sure. The next day we found out that it was *not* cancerous! We were so grateful to God.

As for the convention, it had just begun and things were going great. Like I mentioned earlier, God gave me a totally new team of workers just three months after I took over the conference department, and they were awesome! Suffice it to say, they handled everything—no detail was left undone, and the entire convention went off without a hitch. I must admit I often called from home and begged them for updates. Thankfully, I was able to attend the Friday night session under the influence of some very strong painkillers, but I wouldn't have missed it for anything. I was so proud of my staff!

I spent three long weeks recovering, but it was not wasted time. I was able to pray and read the Word more, as well as watch all my favorite Christian programs on television. I increased in patience! When I finally returned to work, I had a new appreciation for my health and a new compassion for people.

Chapter 10

THE SURPRISE OF MY LIFE

MEETING MY BIRTH MOM

SEASONS CHANGE

I remember it like it was yesterday. The day was August 3, 2005—the day I heard God say, "Seven more months and your season at Joyce Meyer Ministries is over." I was numb. I couldn't even imagine my life not working at JMM, but I knew in my heart, God was speaking to me. Out of obedience to His prompting, I gathered my courage and submitted my resignation. Seven months later, my replacement was hired, and in April of 2006 I said goodbye to Joyce Meyer Ministries, not knowing where I was headed or what was going to happen.

With this major change, our income was immediately cut in half. Consequently, we had to sell our beautiful home on the golf course and move into a two-bedroom apartment nearby. I began to seek God more than ever before. Since He had prompted me to begin writing this book in August of 2000, I assumed it would be nearly finished and I would begin to share my testimony all over the world. That, however, was not what God had in mind.

Instead, He took me into a "wilderness" season for a while. It was so hard. He was so silent. I cried out in prayer for months saying things like, "God! Where are You? What are You doing? I can't stand this silence!" But I heard virtually nothing for well over two years. During that period, many things took place—things I would never have dreamed could happen.

THE MYSTERY BEGINS TO UNFOLD

As I said at the opening, I have always known that I was adopted. But I never made an aggressive attempt to find my birth parents until much later in my life. I made this decision primarily because I didn't want to upset my adoptive mom and dad. Indeed, Mom became very angry at me if I even mentioned it. Out of deep insecurity, she said things like, "What's the matter; aren't we good enough? Haven't we given you everything?" Statements like these almost guaranteed a fight and possibly a spanking, so I just never brought it up.

My dad, on the other hand, was a little less sensitive about the subject and seemed to remember more about my adoption than my mom. Once, I remember him telling me about a piece of paper he saw on the desk of the adoption agency worker with the name Anna Markell Hansen on it. However, he didn't know if that was my birth mother's name or my name. With this small fragment of information, I began to search the Internet. I can't even begin to count how many times I searched online using different variations of that name, looking for my birth mother.

Questions swirled in my mind. I thought, *What does she look like? Does she think of me on my birthday? Does she have other children? Is she somewhere, wanting to meet me? Would she be disappointed if she did? If she and my birth father were never planning to marry, what was her relationship to him? Did they change their minds and get married anyway?* I pondered these questions and many others countless times over the years.

Time passed. It was now 2008 and I was with some friends in Malibu driving to the Los Angeles Dream Center for church on Sunday morning. I just happened to glance out of the window and see a sign for Booth Memorial Hospital. Suddenly, my memory was sparked and I said to them, "Oh! That's where I was born! I have never seen it before." My friends were very familiar with my life story, so one of them quickly looked up Booth Memorial Hospital on the Internet using her phone. Amazingly, she found a website that listed a phone number for adoptees to call if they had been born there and were searching for their birth mothers.

My initial reaction was, *This is too easy*. I had been looking for my birth mother for years but without success. Nevertheless, I wrote the number down and called it when I returned to St. Louis. Much to my surprise, I actually got in touch with someone who thought they could help me. Some agencies charge thousands of dollars to search for birth parents but offer no guarantees. However, the woman I had reached informed me that for a small donation to Booth Memorial Hospital, which was run by the Salvation Army, she would do the search for me. Knowing that the Salvation Army was a reputable organization, I agreed to it. I thought, *Well, even if she doesn't find my birth mother, at least my money is going toward a good cause.*

UNFORSEEN TWISTS ALONG THE WAY

The lady sent me some paperwork to fill out, but I lost it and had to ask her to send it again. Once I sent it in, I virtually forgot about it. Rick's mom became very ill and almost all of our attention focused on her. Within a few weeks she passed away. In the midst of this situation, the woman from the Salvation Army called again and told me she had found three prospects that fit the description of my birth mother. She informed me that she was sending a letter to each of them, asking them to respond to her inquiry about my birth.

Then another unexpected event took place. A few days later, I received a call from my stepsister informing me that my dad was very ill and not expected to live much longer. I desperately wanted a chance to see him again before he passed away. I wanted to tell him that I loved him and make sure he was right with God so that he would go to heaven when he died.

Now, dad was living in Portland, Oregon, but because there were no available flights into Portland, Rick and I flew into Seattle, rented a car and drove south. Thankfully, we had a good visit with him, but I knew I would never see him again until I saw him in heaven.

When we landed back in St. Louis, there was a message on my cell phone from the woman at the Salvation Army. I gave her a call as we drove home from the airport. What she told me would change my life forever. Of the three women she wrote, one had responded and told her she was indeed my birth mother. I screamed and cried and laughed all at the same time. "Are you positive?" I asked her. "Definitely," she said. But here's the "kicker": My birth mother lives in Vancouver, Washington. In other words, when we drove from Seattle to Portland to visit my dad, we drove right past her house! I couldn't believe it!

MAKING CONTACT

The arrangements were made. We were to meet via email. Needless to say, I couldn't sleep. I looked at the first email I wrote for hours before I sent it, making sure it was perfect. The woman who was helping me at the Salvation Army told me that my birth mother was having computer problems and it might be a few days before I heard back from her. "Don't be discouraged," she said. *Are you kidding?* I thought. Every spare moment I had, I checked my email. I even created a separate account, just for her.

One day passed. Two days passed. Three days passed. *Maybe she changed her mind?* I thought. But that was not the case. For one evening when I came home from the gym, it was there—the thing I had been waiting for, praying for and wondering about all my life. It was a message from my birth mom. Kelly. Her name was Kelly. It was short for Markell. My dad was right.

She was amazing! We emailed back and forth for a few days. In one of her messages, she attached a picture of herself with her husband. I stared at it for hours. There she was. I finally knew who I looked like. She was beautiful. She then sent me her phone number, and I could hardly wait to hear her voice. I picked up the phone, and shaking, I dialed the number. She answered—we made contact! Rick and I just sat there and cried. She was real. She was amazing. She was the woman who gave birth to me in August of 1966 at Booth Memorial. It was her…it was really her…and this was really happening.

Meanwhile, two weeks had passed since Rick and I had visited my dad. We received the call we knew was coming: Dad had died. Once the arrangements were made, we flew to Portland for my dad's funeral. Knowing we would be in the area, I made plans to meet with Kelly while we were there. I cannot describe the range of emotions I experienced that week. I had just lost my mother-in-law six weeks earlier; I was about to bury my dad, and the next day I was going to meet Kelly—the woman I had been waiting to meet all my life.

FACE-TO-FACE

I could hardly sleep as a barrage of thoughts ran through my head. *What will I wear? What will I say? Do I hug her? What do I call her?* "Mom" didn't seem right—neither did "mother." I decided on Miss Kelly. I had found her house earlier on Google Earth, so I recognized it immediately as we turned onto her street. There it was. I just sat there and looked at it, knowing she was inside. I got out of the car and told Rick to turn on the camcorder. We walked up the sidewalk and the door opened before I knocked. Face-to-face, we saw each other for the first time and hugged for quite awhile. It was one of the best days of my life.

She told me she was an open book, so I asked her everything I could think of. In the space of a few hours, I got answers to questions I had wondered about my whole life. She said she had always loved me and knew that we would meet one day. That day finally came February 9, 2008.

Time passed, and we celebrated our first Mother's Day together— the first of many to come. We keep in touch regularly. I have tried many times to understand how all this happened. *Why now?* I questioned. *Why after my parents were gone? Would it have been too painful for them to know that I had found her?* I will probably never know the answers to these questions, but what I do know is that God heard and answered my prayer. It wasn't as quickly as I would have liked, but He did answer it. I can only imagine the smile on His face, knowing how happy He has made me. He is my Abba Daddy God, and it is His joy to give us the desires of our heart!

CONCLUSION

A FINAL WORD

MY PRESENT POSITION

Once my adoptive parents were gone and I was reunited with my birth mother, I thought, *Now! Now, the book will be finished. Of course, I had to meet my birth mother!* However, that was not the case. Several months passed, and God threw me another curve ball. I was working at Gold's Gym in Fenton, Missouri, because we needed some additional income and I really wanted to get back in shape.

I started out working behind the front desk but soon transferred to sales. Wow, was that a change from working in full-time ministry! But it was actually very good for me because it helped me become bolder than I had ever been in sharing my testimony. Time and again, I told my story to someone and then sold them a gym membership with personal training! The opportunities God gave me were truly amazing.

In September 2008, however, I knew that my season of employment at Gold's Gym was over. The book was finally nearing completion and I felt the time was drawing near for me to prepare for its release. I thought I would have a bit of a respite, but again, I was wrong. God had other plans, but He hadn't revealed them to me yet. Instead, He revealed them to Rick, which really kind of ticked me off.

Keep in mind, Rick was (and still is) working as the Distribution Department manager at Joyce Meyer Ministries. He came home from work one day with a job description for an opening at the St.

Louis Dream Center. It was the position of executive assistant/office supervisor. When he first told me about it, I was very angry with him. I didn't want to get just another job—I wanted *the job* that was God's will. But Rick said in his usual tone, "Honey, just pray about it. There's something about this; I don't know what it is. Just pray about it, okay?"

"Fine!" I retorted. So I reluctantly prayed about it, and the moment I said to God, "If You want me to go, I'll go," He spoke to me and said that it was indeed what He wanted me to do. Although it made absolutely no sense to me, I chose to obey.

So here I am—presently and blissfully employed at the St. Louis Dream Center. We are feeding the hungry, clothing the naked and sharing the Gospel with the poor and needy of St. Louis. Victoria and Christian are growing physically, spiritually and academically as they work through their high school years, and our family is serving the Lord together in a church that's on fire for Him. I couldn't be happier!

A NEW APPRECIATION FOR GOD

I believe by now that you have an idea of how grateful I am to God for all He has done in my life. In spite of all the things I've done and all the places I've been, He never left me and He never gave up on me. When everyone else had forsaken me, He remained faithful to me. Even when I was in the depth of sin, He stayed right by me.

I will never forget the night God spoke to me and gave me a greater revelation of what He had done in my life. It was very late and I was laying in bed, thanking God for all He had done. An overwhelming sense of gratitude flooded my soul, and I began to express my deep appreciation to Him for delivering me from drug addiction, lust, seducing spirits, prostitution, and many other bondages. In His gentle and unique way, the Lord spoke to me and said, "Yeah, I changed 'Pepper' into *salt*" (see Matthew 5:13). God is so good!

I hope that you can see how head-over-heels in love I am with Jesus. He made it all possible, and that is why I will serve Him all the days of my life. That is also why I titled this book *From Vegas to Victory: The Death of a Prostitute.* 'Pepper' is dead because she is the woman I was in my former life. And Judy Lamborn has been born again by the Spirit of God to be salt to the earth and light to the world. I have always loved Jesus, but now I *appreciate* Him. I appreciate the fact that He delivered me from cigarettes, drugs, alcohol and prostitution. I appreciate the fact that He helped me clean up my mouth. And I appreciate the fact that He transformed me into a godly woman who seeks after His heart.

I have told the Lord many times that there is nothing I wouldn't do for Him because He has done so much for me. It wasn't easy writing this book, but He asked me to do it and gave me the grace to complete it. I believe it will go all over the world and be a blessing to multiplied millions of people.

My heart's cry is for all that I am and everything I do to bring praise and worship to the Lord. I deeply desire all my thoughts, words, attitudes, and actions to be well pleasing to Him. I do not want Jesus' death to be in vain in my life. I want to fulfill His perfect will for Judy Lamborn.

MY PRAYER FOR YOU

Let me encourage you by saying God is not a respecter of persons. Everything that you have read in this book that He has delivered me from or blessed me with, He is willing to do for *you* and anyone else who seeks and trusts Him.

My prayer for you is that my testimony of God's unconditional love and saving grace will touch your heart and draw you closer to Him. I pray that you are encouraged not to give up, in spite of any difficult circumstance or situation you are facing. God has an awesome plan for your life! In Hebrews 13:5 it says, ...*[God] Himself has said, I will not in any way fail you nor give you up nor leave you without support. [I will] not, [I will] not, [I will] not in any degree leave you helpless not forsake nor let [you] down (relax My hold on you)! [Assuredly not!]* (AMP) I pray that you personally experience the unsearchable, immeasurable richness of His unconditional love.

His love is what drew me. His love is what motivates me. His love is what sustains me.

If you have never asked God to forgive you of your sins and invited Jesus, His Son, to become the Lord of your life, I urge you to do so. Likewise, if you have not received the promised gift of the Father, the baptism of the Holy Spirit, I highly recommend you do. I have included both a prayer of salvation and a prayer to be baptized in the Holy Spirit at the end of this book. I have also included a list of recommended resources regarding some of the people who have ministered to me over the years.

My friend, **God loves you!** Don't push Him away any longer. He longs to be invited into every area of your life; He yearns to fellowship and spend time with you *every day*. Jesus died a horrible death on a cross and shed His blood so that you could be free. Come to Him with a humble heart… Ask Him to forgive you of your sins and invite Him into your life today… His arms are opened wide… He will not turn you away!

****

If God has used my testimony to touch and change your life, I would love to hear from you and learn what He is doing. I have included my address for you to send your testimonies and prayer requests. I can assure you that if you send me a prayer request, we will pray and believe God for your miracle.

Your sister in Christ,
Judy

PRAYER OF SALVATION

God is waiting for you right now…

It's not difficult to talk to Him…

He knows everything about you…The Bible says He knows how many hairs are on your head…He cares about you….and, He doesn't have favorites—what He did for me, He will do for you.

Don't pretend or try to act "holy" (He doesn't like that anyway), but rely on the Bible to help you to understand what it really means to be holy.

He made you to be you— just like you are…

Here's what I did—feel free to use this prayer or just talk to God in your own words…

"God, I have really messed up my life. I know I am a sinner. I need your help. Please forgive me for the sins that I have committed against You. I believe that Your Son, Jesus, died a horrible death on a cross and shed His blood so that I can be saved from an eternity in Hell. I don't want to go to Hell. I want to go to Heaven and I know that accepting

Jesus as my Savior is the only way to make that happen. Jesus, I accept you as my Savior, come into my heart and be my Lord. I want to be saved. I want to be a child of God. I give my life completely over to You. I renounce my former lifestyle and from this day forward I am going to live my life for You."

That's it. Simple, right?

If you prayed that prayer and meant it in your heart, you just took the first step towards a brighter future…feels good, doesn't it…

PRAYER FOR THE BAPTISM OF THE HOLY SPIRIT

I realize this is a controversial issue; however I simply cannot deny what this has done in my life. Initially I was very skeptical about the whole "speaking in tongues" thing, but it's real. And it's powerful. It's better than any drug induced high I have ever been on.

Receiving the fullness of the Holy Spirit is just as easy as receiving Jesus as your Savior and Lord. You simply ask. That's all. It's a free gift that God is waiting to give you. All you have to do is unwrap it! Are you ready? Then let's go!

There are a few prerequisites to be being baptized in the Holy Spirit. First and foremost, you must have already received Jesus Christ as your Savior and Lord. (See John 14.17)

Secondly, you can't have regular patterns of disobedience in your life. Acts 5:32 says that God gives His Spirit "to those who obey Him." This is particularly true of unforgiveness. If you are holding unforgiveness towards someone, forgive them right now. You can't do anything to change what they did to you. Holding unforgiveness towards someone gives them power over you. Don't give in to that. Let it go. The Bible says in Matthew 6:15 that if you don't forgive people when they sin against you, God will not forgive you of your sins. So you're not forgiving them for their sake, you're forgiving them for your sake. If you are struggling with this, pray this simple prayer:

> *Father, I ask that You would search me and show me if there is any disobedience in my*

> *heart. Please show me if there is any person*
> *I have withheld forgiveness from. I want to*
> *obey and forgive no matter what You reveal*
> *to me. I ask this in the name of Jesus.*

Once you prayer that prayer, sit quietly for a few minutes and allow God to show you who you need to forgive. Chances are, you already know…If you can't find the words to say, pray this:

> *"Father as an act of my will, I forgive*
> *_____(say their name aloud). I*
> *am asking you to help my emotions catch*
> *up with this decision I have made.*
> *_____(say their name aloud*
> *again) I forgive you and I release you."*

Read Luke 11:11-13. God is desiring to give this good gift to you. All you have to do is ask. You must ask in faith though. Don't doubt. (James 1:6-7) I live in Missouri, also known as the "Show Me" state because people here don't believe anything unless you show them first. Well, that attitude is not an attitude of faith. An attitude of faith says, "I believe I receive the moment I ask." (Mark 11:24) Remember, believe then receive.

Acts 2:4 says they all were filled with the Holy Spirit and began to speak with other tongues as the Spirit gave them utterance. Notice they did the speaking. Not the Holy Spirit. What do you have to do if you want to speak? You have to move your lips, your tongue and your vocal cords. So you are going to be doing something when you receive. Contrary to what some may think, the Holy Spirit is not going to grab your lips, tongue and vocal chords and make you speak. You must speak or yield to Him as He gives you the utterance.

When you ask to receive the baptism of the Holy Spirit, you may have a syllable bubble up or roll around in your head. If you will simply speak that out in faith, it will be like a dam breaking open and your supernatural prayer language will come. Even if it's only one syllable, speak it out. Don't let the devil (or anyone else) convince you it's not real. He'll try to tell you "You sound ridiculous." Well, he's a liar who can't speak the truth even if he wanted to. He knows how dangerous you will become to him when you receive this gift.

Remember, you can pray in tongues whenever you want to. It's like a water fountain. The water is always there; you just have to turn the knob and out comes the water. So pray in tongues as often as you can.

Now, are you ready? If you believe you will receive, let's pray this together. One last thing: you can't speak in English and Spanish simultaneously. Same thing with speaking in tongues; you can't pray in English and pray in tongues at the same time. Just yield yourself to the Holy Spirit. Let's pray:

> *Father, in the name of Jesus, I come to you as Your child. You said if I asked You for the Holy Spirit You would give Him to me. With joy I now ask in faith; please baptize and fill me at this very moment with You Holy Spirit. I receive all You have for me including the ability to speak in tongues. So now in faith I will speak in new tongues! Amen!*

RECOMMENDED RESOURCES

These are some of the people that God used to help me grow up and mature in my relationship with Him. Their teaching material is located on their respective websites.

Dave & Joyce Meyer – www.joycemeyer.org

John & Lisa Bevere – www.messengerinternational.org

Dave Roberson – www.daveroberson.org

Kenneth & Gloria Copeland – www.kcm.org

Jesse & Cathy Duplantis – www.jdm.org

Norvel Hayes – www.nhm.cc

Paula White – www.paulawhite.org

Keith Moore – www.moorelife.org

Creflo & Taffi Dollar – www.creflodollarministries.org

Stormie Omartian – www.stormieomartian.com

Dutch Sheets – www.dutchsheets.org

Rick & Denise Renner – www.renner.org

ABOUT THE AUTHOR

Judy Lamborn was born in 1966 in Los Angeles, California, where she was adopted at four months old. From the time she grew up as a child in California and Iowa to the years she spent working in a brothel in Las Vegas, Judy's life was filled with abuse, turbulence and fear.

By the grace of God, she eventually broke free from drugs, alcohol and prostitution, got married, and began her new life in 1991 which included Christ at the helm. In 1998, Judy and her family moved to St. Louis, Missouri, where she began working for Joyce Meyer Ministries.

Judy's testimony proves that dreams do come true, and that God's grace and mercy can raise any individual from a low place to a high place. Judy started off with Joyce Meyer Ministries in the call center in 1998 and was eventually promoted to conference department manager in April 2000, overseeing 25 to 30 meetings a year with thousands in attendance, both in the United States and overseas. She is presently working as an executive assistant/office supervisor at the St. Louis Dream Center, the inner city outreach of Joyce Meyer Ministries. Her husband, Rick, also works for Joyce Meyer Ministries as manager of the distribution department. Judy and Rick still reside in St. Louis with their two children, Victoria and Christian, and their beloved English bulldog, Daisy Duke.

Through Judy's testimony and through the establishment of Redeeming Love Ministries, she has seen many people set free from drug addiction, pornography, prostitution, and the guilt and shame following abortion. Her story has been broadcast twice to millions of viewers on Joyce Meyer television programs. And Judy is also looking forward to sharing her story to millions more through her media appearances, speaking engagements, and her first book—*From Vegas to Victory: The Death of a Prostitute.*

You can contact Judy Lamborn at:

Redeeming Love Ministries
476 Old Smizer Mill Road #234
Fenton, Missouri 63026

Telephone:
(636) 671-7170

www.judylamborn.com

Email:
ytasno@gmail.com

CPSIA information can be obtained at www.ICGtesting.com
Printed in the USA
LVOW090022041111

253416LV00003B/4/P